ItsDeductible™

Taxpayer Name _____

Taxpayer Social Security Number _____

Important Copyright Information

This workbook is copyrighted and can be used only by one taxpayer and only for the tax year 2002. Any other use of this workbook is prohibited by law. Retain and store this workbook with your 2002 tax return records.

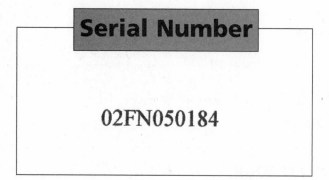

Serial Number

02FN050184

Be sure to register <u>today</u> using the card in the back of this workbook (Page 145)
Or at <u>www.ItsDeductible.com</u> - click on REGISTER NOW

©2002 Income Dynamics, Inc. All Rights Reserved 800-976-5358 ISBN 0-9653626-3-9

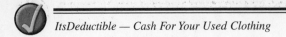
TABLE OF CONTENTS

©2002 Income Dynamics, Inc.   All Rights Reserved   800-976-5358   ISBN 0-9653626-3-9

How ItsDeductible™ Works!

Deduct the Full Value of Your Donated Items

ItsDeductible™ is a revolutionary product that enables you to properly value your non-cash donations such as used clothing, toys or other household goods, so you can deduct the actual fair-market-value and receive the full deduction when itemizing your taxes.

Determining the Fair-Market-Value of Your Items

Every year, millions of taxpayers give away bags of clothing and other items to charity, yet the vast majority of these taxpayers miss out on tax savings to which they are legally entitled because they do not know how much their donation is worth. *ItsDeductible*™ helps you take advantage of the full, legal deduction, saving hundreds of dollars on your taxes each year by providing actual fair-market-values of thousands of commonly donated items.

IRS Guidelines

IRS publications 526 and 561 both state that it is our legal right to deduct the "fair-market-value" of donated items. However, the IRS does not provide a guide to help taxpayers value their donations and suggests taxpayers compare their donated items to a few similar items in thrift and consignment stores to get an indication of their fair market value. Because of the time and effort involved, most taxpayers simply choose not to do this and therefore miss out on one of the most significant tax deductions available today. That is where *ItsDeductible*™ can help!

How We Determine Values

Using patent pending Intelligent Indexing™ technology to capture millions of internet transactions, combined with a nation-wide network of manual data collection, *ItsDeductible*™ has organized and compiled this data into a powerful set of tools that accurately applies the fair-market-value to thousands of commonly donated items. Each item is given a specific value, based on condition, age, and market demand. This translates directly into tax savings.

What This Workbook Will Do For You!

1. Help you determine how much all those items you donate to charity are really worth!

2. Give you a quick and easy way to track and assign values to each of your donated items!

3. Increase your tax deduction by properly valuing your donation and increasing the amount you can deduct.

4. Save you hundreds of dollars on your income taxes.

5. Provide an organized and comprehensive record of your donations and related values for future reference.

6. Help you benefit your favorite charities by giving them valuable donations while taking full advantage of the tax break to which you are entitled!

Who Can Benefit From ItsDeductible™?

- Are you running out of storage space?
- Has any member of your household outgrown their clothes?
- Is your closet packed full of clothes that are outdated or haven't been worn in the past year?
- Does your garage need a good cleaning?
- Are you interested in saving additional tax dollars and getting a bigger tax refund this year?

Wouldn't it be nice to receive some cash for those unwanted but perfectly usable items of clothing and household goods that overwhelm your storage space? Then you need ItsDeductible™!

Why Not a Garage Sale?

Chances are you've had a garage sale to get back some of the money you spent on your family's clothes and household goods. Garage sales, unfortunately, involve the expense of advertising and signs, and the time to mark, sort and price every item.

Add to that sitting for hours in the hot sun with strangers parading in and out of your garage. Plus the fact that most items sell for fifty-cents to a dollar. **Wouldn't it be much easier to simply donate these items to your favorite charity?**

Donate It Instead

And Start Turning Donations Into Dollars With ItsDeductible™!

Believe it or not, donating clothes and other household goods can generate cash too - often much, much more than you could generate at a garage sale. By donating your items to a qualified charitable organization and deducting that donation on your income tax return, you will benefit those less fortunate while also receiving a significant tax break.

What most people don't realize is that their donated items are usually worth a lot more than they think! A recent survey showed that more than 90% of people who donate non-cash items to charity underestimate the value of their donated items by as much as 300% — simply because they do not know the fair-market-value of these items. When you use this workbook, you'll be able to instantly assign the actual fair-market-value to thousands of commonly donated items.

Here's an example of how *ItsDeductible*™ can increase your tax savings simply by applying proper values to the items you donate:

WITHOUT ItsDeductible™

Donated to Charity
- 3 bags of clothes
- dresser
- lawn mower

Your Estimated Value	**$300**
Tax Savings	**$108**

WITH ItsDeductible™

Donated Items	Number	Value	Total
Girls Blouses and Shirts	12-Fair	$ 6	$ 72
Girls Casual Dresses	8-Good	$ 15	$ 120
Mens Designer Silk Ties	8-Fair	$ 8	$ 64
Mens Designer Dress Winter Coat	1-Fair	$ 100	$ 100
Womens Long Formal	2-Good	$ 120	$ 240
Mens Designer V-neck Sweaters	4-Good	$ 35	$ 140
Mens Designer Two Piece Suits	1-Good	$ 390	$ 390
Women's Casual Dresses	3-Fair	$ 15	$ 45
Men's Designer Long Sleeve Shirts	3-Poor	$ 10	$ 30
Mens Pull Over Sweaters	4-Good	$ 20	$ 80
Dresser	1-Good	$ 169	$ 169
Lawn Mower	1-Good	$ 165	$ 165

Actual Value Using Cash for Your Used Clothing	**$1,615**
Tax Savings	**$581**

ADDITIONAL SAVINGS: $473 (Assumes 36% Tax Bracket)

ItsDeductible™ also provides you with worksheets to track and deduct out-of-pocket expenses, mileage expense, and cash donations. Keep this workbook handy throughout the year and use it whenever you make a donation to charity. Consider it your comprehensive donation guide and tracking tool.

Be sure to save your receipts and other documentation and place in the handy folder in the back of this workbook. Then simply file this workbook along with your taxes for future reference.

How Much Can You Save?

The full fair-market-value of your donations can be deducted when you itemize on your tax return. That's why it is so important to properly value the items you donate.

The deduction calculated by *ItsDeductible™* reduces the amount of your taxable income, which in-turn reduces the amount of taxes you must pay to the federal government and to some state governments.

AN ILLUSTRATION OF HOW MUCH YOU CAN SAVE	
Value of Sample Donation	$1,500.00
Sample Federal and State Tax Rate	33%
Your Tax Savings	$495.00

How much you save will vary depending on your *marginal tax rate.* The marginal tax rate is the percentage of your income (over a base amount) that you pay in taxes.

Don't Wait For Your Refund!

It's great to think of getting a bigger tax refund next April, but if you don't want to wait for your tax refund you don't have to! Ask your employer for a new W-4 Withholding Form and simply increase the number of your exemptions.

As a general guideline, if your total donations for the year approaches $2,700, claim one *additional* exemption on your W-4 form.

This reduces the amount of tax withheld from your paycheck each pay period, providing you with tax savings throughout the entire year.

Getting Started On Your Tax Savings

Getting started is sometimes the hardest part of any task. However, knowing how much you can gain by cleaning out that cluttered closet or garage can be a great incentive!

Begin by cleaning out one closet. Sort similar items into piles on the bed: shirts, pants, dresses, etc. Snap a photograph! Then use the following pages to record each item according to the proper category.

Place items into boxes or large plastic bags and call the charity to pick them up - or drive them there yourself. (Remember to deduct your mileage!) Be sure to save the receipt(s) given to you by the charity. They will not provide values for your items, but this receipt will serve as evidence that the items you list in this workbook were donated.

> Hint: Use "HASH" marks when you have more than
>   one item in a particular category.

> Hint: If you use the workbook later in the year for recording
>   additional clothing donations, use a different color ink.

Figure your tax savings immediately and file an amended W-4 with your employer to receive your money over the balance of the year (see page 8), or wait until the end of the year after all your donations have been made. Now, think of all the things you can do with your tax windfall:

- Start planning for your future and invest your savings!
- Start a college savings fund for your children or grandchildren!
- Contribute more to your IRA or start a new IRA!
- Contribute to an organization that is important to you!
- Take a vacation!
- Buy new clothes (don't forget to donate them to charity when they become old or outdated)!

And then - why not clean out another closet? Or the basement? Maybe even the garage? You will truly be amazed at the impact when you begin turning donations into dollars with *ItsDeductible™!*

Making Item Donations

Choose A Qualified Organization

Some simple guidelines will help you obtain maximum tax benefits when giving away used clothing and household goods.

You must give your items to a qualified 501 (c)(3) organization. Some of those that qualify are:

- Amvets
- Boy & Girl Scouts
- Goodwill
- Churches/Synagogues
- Council of the Blind
- Disabled American Veterans
- Federal, State & Local Governments
- Public Parks and Recreation
- Red Cross
- Salvation Army
- Society for the Deaf
- Tax-exempt educational institutions
- Tax-exempt hospitals

If you have any questions about an organization's tax status, contact the organization directly and ask if they qualify for tax-exempt status.

Some thrift organizations will even come to your home to pick up your donated items.

For a complete listing of qualified organizations, you can visit our web site at **www.ItsDeductible.com** and do a direct link to this information provided by the IRS.

Valuing Your Donated Items

In order to accurately determine your tax deduction, you will need to assign a value to the items you donate. According to the Internal Revenue Service, a taxpayer can deduct the fair-market-value of clothing, toys, household goods, used furniture, shoes, books, or any item you donate to a qualified charity. IRS Publication 561 states that the fair-market-value is determined as "the price that would be agreed upon between a willing buyer and a willing seller, with neither being required to act, and both having reasonable knowledge of the relevant facts."

ItsDeductible™ has established the fair-market-values for you, through carefully following IRS guidelines. Using patent-pending Intelligent Indexing™ technology, combined with a nation-wide network of manual data collection, *ItsDeductible™* has organized and compiled this data into a powerful set of tools that accurately applies the fair market values to thousands of commonly donated items. Each item is given a specific value in a range including High, Average, and Low, which translates directly into tax savings.

Determining the Value Category

The Certified Market Valuation Section provides you with worksheets in which to indicate the Value Category and Quantity of each item you donate. The charity will not provide item values for you. Using *ItsDeductible™*, however, makes this process quick and easy.

The value of an item is often affected by the condition of that item. For example, a suit worn only a couple of times with no apparent wear would be valued higher than one that shows noticeable wear.

As a result of our research and analysis we have grouped items into three categories, **"High," "Average"** or **"Low"**.

Because the primary indicator is often condition, the following guideline may be helpful:

HIGH

An item in good condition that shows no noticeable wear or defects.

AVERAGE

An item in fair condition that shows slight wear or defects.

LOW

An item in poor condition that shows appreciable wear or defects.

Other Factors That Affect Item Values

There are additional factors which affect the value of donated items. According to IRS Publication 561, these factors would include, desirability, use, and scarcity. These factors have been taken into account in the numbers presented within the workbook, and must also be considered when you are assigning values to items not listed in the workbook (Custom Items).

Important: It is important to note that *ItsDeductible*™ serves as a guideline to assist you in establishing the value of your donated items. The IRS expects taxpayers to make a "good faith effort" when determining the value of your donated items. The taxpayer is ultimately responsible for assigning the Value Category and must be able to substantiate their decision.

Designer Brands

Designer and/or upscale name-brand apparel and accessories carry a higher fair market value due to the quality and craftsmanship, and are listed beginning on page 45 of this workbook.

Examples of Designer and Name-Brand Clothing:

• Bill Blass	• Ralph Lauren	• DKNY
• Hugo Boss	• Polo	• Nautica
• Giorgio Armani	• Guess	• Perry Ellis
• Coach	• Tommy Hilfiger	• Johnston & Murphy
• Liz Claiborne	• Calvin Klein	• Nine West
• Jones New York	• Dior	• Ann Taylor
• Chaus	• Yves St. Laurent	

Other Charitable Donations

Out-of-Pocket Expenses

Out-of-pocket donations are described as expenses incurred while perform-ing volunteer charitable work, or as a function of participation in or with a tax-exempt organization.

Some examples include:

- Buying doughnuts for a church youth group
- Purchasing movie tickets for a Boy Scouts troop outing
- Buying an airline ticket for travel on a mission trip
- Purchasing Sunday School materials or literature
- Taking someone to lunch to discuss fund-raising

Fund-raising events may also be considered an out-of-pocket donation, however, certain restrictions apply.

Fund-Raising Events

Have you ever wondered if you could deduct the cost of a ticket to a charity event, or the cost of something you bought at a charity auction or bazaar? Parts of those costs are deductible if the price you paid is more than the benefit you received.

Some examples:

- If you paid $40 for a ticket to attend a charity auction, and the price includes a meal valued at $15, you can deduct the difference of $25 as a charitable donation.
- If you paid $100 for an item at a charity auction and the item had a fair market value of $60, you can deduct the remaining $40.
- If you make a contribution of more than $75 to a qualified organiza-tion that is partly for goods or services you receive, the organization must give you a written statement.

Charities are now required to state the deductible amount of your contribu-tion on the face of the ticket. Be sure to retain the ticket for your records. In some instances, you may be able to deduct 100% of the cost. Check our website at **www.ItsDeductible.com** and click Deduction Information for more information.

Monetary Donations

Monetary Donations are donations made to a charitable organization in the form of cash, check, credit card or debit card.

Whether an individual places a $20 bill in a church offering or pledges $100 to the American Cancer Association, the transaction can be logged and managed in this portion of *ItsDeductible™*. The Monetary Donations section allows for convenient tracking of monthly or annual donations. Tracking includes payment method to include specific credit card or check number used for the donation.

Mileage Expense

Travel costs are deductible as a charitable donation when they are not reimbursed by the charity. The current IRS mileage deduction is 14 cents per mile. Toll and parking fees can be deducted in addition to the 14-cent mileage deduction.

- Volunteering for administrative duties at a local church
- Delivering clothing donations to a charity
- Vacation Bible School
- Meals on Wheels
- Coaching sports teams sponsored by tax exempt organizations (churches, city recreation departments, youth sports, etc)
- Religious or school-related activities, such as youth field trips or driving children to Scout or church camp

NOTE: No deduction is allowed if there is any significant personal pleasure, vacation or recreation involved in the travel for charity.

A Note About Donated Automobiles

The IRS has released a Service Center Advice memorandum that discusses the valuation method to be used in valuing automobiles given to a charitable organization. It indicates that the fair market value of the vehicle is the amount that a willing buyer would pay a willing seller, when each has relevant knowledge of the facts. The fair market value can be established by using car guidebooks such as the Kelly Blue Book or the National Automobile Dealer's Association Used Car Guide. For Internet users, you can visit our website at **www.ItsDeductible.com** and link to the Kelly Blue Book for used car values.

Some charitable activities that could result in tax deductions for using your vehicle are:

- Volunteering for administrative duties at your church
- Delivering clothing donations to a charity
- Religious - or school-related activities, such as youth field trips or driving children to Scout or church camp
- Volunteering to spend time with children at school, or taking students out to eat
- Vacation Bible School
- Meals on Wheels
- Coaching sports teams sponsored by tax exempt organizations (for example, churches, city recreation departments, youth sports, etc.)

You may be surprised how quickly the miles can add up.

No deduction is allowed, however, if there is any significant personal pleasure, vacation or recreation involved in the travel for charity.

Non-Deductible Donations

Some charity-related transactions are not deductible:

- Purchasing but not using tickets to a charitable event. This is because you have purchased a privilege, whether or not you used it.
- Paying fair market value for an item at a charity auction. The price you paid must exceed the item's value in order for the difference to be deductible.
- Blood donations to the Red Cross or blood banks (however, mileage is deductible).
- Payment to a college or university where the tax donor receives a right to buy seating at an athletic event (even in a sky box) is 80% deductible as a contribution. No amount paid for the tickets themselves is deductible.
- Buying tickets for charity raffles, lotteries, bingo or similar drawings for valuable prizes is not deductible whether you win a prize or not.
- The value of income lost while you work as an unpaid volunteer for a qualified organization.

Other Charitable Deductions

If you do volunteer work for a charity or church and have to spend some of your own money or use your own vehicle, you can deduct your actual expenses. However, you cannot deduct the value of your services, your knowledge or your time.

Record Keeping

Four Simple Steps To Follow

1. Indicate the quantity and value category on the certified market value section, then tally your extended total.
2. Record the names and addresses of the organizations receiving your donations on page 132.
3. Arrange your items on the floor, sofa or bed and take a quick snapshot or video. While this is not required, it will substantiate your contribution if questions ever arise. Keep the visual *record with your personal tax records.* Do not include them with your tax return. *(If you have already donated your goods and did not take a photo, simply skip this step.)*
4. When making your donation, obtain a SIGNED, DATED receipt for your donations. Your donation must be made by December 31, 2002 in order to claim this donation on your 2002 tax return.

You are not required to have a receipt where it is impractical to get one (for example, if you leave property at a charity's unattended drop site). Just document this fact in the back of the workbook.

The Omnibus Budget Reconciliation Act of 1993 states that a taxpayer must substantiate any contribution of $250 or more at the time of the donation with a written acknowledgment from the organization, unless the organization files a statement with the IRS that contains the required information. Most, however, do not file this information, so you need to obtain a signed dated receipt of your donation.

> Tip: You can record multiple donations throughout the year by designating each donation with a different color of ink.

Rules to Follow

Like all tax matters, there are a few rules concerning charitable donations.

If your donation of clothing and household goods is more than $500, Form 8283 must be filed with your tax return. All information needed to complete Form 8283 is included in this workbook. As long as the value of the donated item or group of similar items does not exceed $5,000, an outside appraisal is not required.

> **Similar Items of Property:** Similar items of property are items of the same generic category or type, such as stamp collections, coin collections, lithographs, paintings, books, non-publicly traded stock, land or buildings.
>
> > *Example:* You claimed a deduction of $2,100 for clothing and $6,000 for a collection of books. Report the clothing in Section A of Form 8283 and the books (a group of similar items, which requires an appraisal) in Section B of Form 8283.

Most donated clothing and household items will not be worth more than you paid for them. If you have owned an item for less than one year, the most you can deduct is the amount you paid for it. If you owned an item for more than one year, you can deduct the current fair-market-value for that item, even if the fair-market-value is more than the amount you paid.

There are instances when your property may have increased in value. For detailed information, refer to IRS Publication 561, "Determining the Value of Donated Property".

Examples of determining that actual value of donated items:

> *Example 1:* A pair of men's jeans in good condition, (no noticeable wear), are worth $19 as a deduction. However, if you only paid $16 for those jeans six months ago, the most you can deduct is $16.
>
> *Example 2:* If you have a six-month-old coffee maker but it's in poor condition, then you must select the low-value-category and take only the $1 deduction.
>
> *Example 3:* If you buy a designer leather purse in good condition for $20 at a garage sale and 15 months later you donate this purse to charity in fair condition, then you can deduct $45, the fair-market-value for this item, in accordance with IRS guidelines.

Federal Income Tax Brackets For 2002

Tax Rate	Married	Single
10%	Under $12,000	Under $6000
15%	$12,001 - $46,700	$6,001 - $27,950
27%	$46,701 - $112,850	$27,951 - $67,700
30%	$112,851 - $171,950	$67,701 - $141,250
35%	$171,951 - $307,050	$141,251 - $307,050
38.6%	$307,051 and above	$307,051 and above

In other words, if you are married and your taxable income is from $46,701 to $112,850, you are in the 27 percent tax bracket and every $100 in deductions saves you $27 in federal taxes. ($100.00 x 27% = $27.00)

You save even more if you pay state income taxes. The marginal tax rate in many states averages 6%, or an additional $6 saved for every $100 in donations. This would mean a total savings of $33 for every $100 worth of donations.

For Example: $27.00 Federal Tax Savings
+ $6.00 State Tax Savings
$33.00 Total Tax Savings

Using Tax Form 8283

1. You must complete Form 8283 when the value of your donated items is more than $500.
2. If you would like to print a copy of Form 8283 or any other IRS form, you can visit our website at **www.ItsDeductible.com** and do a direct link to this IRS site for printing forms.

Sample Tax Form 8283:

Form **8283** (Rev. October 1998) Department of the Treasury Internal Revenue Service

Noncash Charitable Contributions

▶ Attach to your tax return if you claimed a total deduction of over $500 for all contributed property.

▶ See separate instructions.

OMB No. 1545-0908

Attachment Sequence No. **55**

Name(s) shown on your income tax return | **Identifying number**

Note: *Figure the amount of your contribution deduction before completing this form. See your tax return instructions.*

Section A– List in this section **only** items (or groups of similar items) for which you claimed a deduction of $5,000 or less. Also, list certain publicly traded securities even if the deduction is over $5,000 (see instructions).

Part I **Information on Donated Property–** If you need more space, attach a statement.

1	(a) Name and address of the donee organization	(b) Description of donated property
A		
B		
C		
D		
E		

Note: *If the amount you claimed as a deduction for an item is $500 or less, you do not have to complete columns (d), (e), and (f).*

	(c) Date of the contribution	(d) Date acquired by donor (mo., yr.)	(e) How acquired by donor	(f) Donor's cost or adjusted basis	(g) Fair market value	(h) Method used to determine the fair market value
A						
B						
C						
D						
E						

Part II **Other Information–** Complete line 2 if you gave less than an entire interest in property listed in Part I. Complete line 3 if conditions were attached to a contribution listed in Part I.

2 If, during the year, you contributed less than the entire interest in the property, complete lines a–e.

a Enter the letter from Part I that identifies the property ▶ ______. If Part II applies to more than one property, attach a separate statement.

b Total amount claimed as a deduction for the property listed in Part I: **(1)** For this tax year ▶ ______. **(2)** For any prior tax years ▶ ______.

c Name and address of each organization to which any such contribution was made in a prior year (complete only if different from the donee organization above):

Name of charitable organization (donee)

Address (number, street, and room or suite no.)

City or town, state, and ZIP code

d For tangible property, enter the place where the property is located or kept ▶ ______

e Name of any person, other than the donee organization, having actual possession of the property ▶ ______

3 If conditions were attached to any contribution listed in Part I, answer questions a – c and attach the required statement (see instructions).

	Yes	No
a Is there a restriction, either temporary or permanent, on the donee's right to use or dispose of the donated property?		
b Did you give to anyone (other than the donee organization or another organization participating with the donee organization in cooperative fundraising) the right to the income from the donated property or to the possession of the property, including the right to vote donated securities, to acquire the property by purchase or otherwise, or to designate the person having such income, possession, or right to acquire?		
c Is there a restriction limiting the donated property for a particular use?		

For Paperwork Reduction Act Notice, see page 4 of separate instructions. Cat. No. 62299J Form **8283** (Rev. 10-98)

Page **2**

Identifying number

r items) for which you claimed a contributions of certain publicly

the **Note** in Part I below.

nd/or appraiser.

lry ☐ Stamp Collections ☐ Other

ative arts, textiles, carpets, silver, rare

he signed appraisal. See instructions.

hary of the overall ft | (c) Appraised fair market value

See instructions

claimed as a duction | (i) Average trading price of securities

that the appraisal identifies as ructions.

appraised value of not more than $500

Date ▶

property, employed by, or related to any if regularly used by the donor, donee, or

is; and that because of my qualifications fy that the appraisal fees were not based overstatement of the property value as section 6701(a) (aiding and abetting the y by the Director of Practice.

ate of appraisal ▶

Identifying number

ion.

)(c) and that it received the donated

of the property described in Section B, Part I (or any portion thereof) within 2 years after the date of receipt, it will file **Form 8282**, Donee Information Return, with the IRS and give the donor a copy of that form. This acknowledgment does not represent agreement with the claimed fair market value.

Does the organization intend to use the property for an unrelated use? ▶ ☐ Yes ☐ No

Name of charitable organization (donee)	**Employer identification number**	
Address (number, street, and room or suite no.)	City or town, state, and ZIP code	
Authorized signature	Title	Date

Women's Clothing

Description	High* Good Condition	Average* Fair Condition	Low* Poor Condition	Total
Accessories				
Belts				
Leather	_____ $15.00	_____ $6.00	_____ $1.00	_____
Other	_____ $10.00	_____ $4.00	_____ $1.00	_____
Gloves				
Casual	_____ $10.00	_____ $4.00	_____ $1.00	_____
Dress	_____ $10.00	_____ $4.00	_____ $1.00	_____
Mittens	_____ $5.00	_____ $3.00	_____ $1.00	_____
Purses				
Dress	_____ $38.00	_____ $10.00	_____ $1.00	_____
Leather	_____ $47.00	_____ $12.00	_____ $1.00	_____
Other	_____ $15.00	_____ $8.00	_____ $1.00	_____
Scarves				
Dress	_____ $12.00	_____ $5.00	_____ $1.00	_____
Other	_____ $6.00	_____ $3.00	_____ $1.00	_____
Blouses and Shirts				
Casual				
Long-Sleeve	_____ $16.00	_____ $8.00	_____ $3.00	_____
Short-Sleeve	_____ $15.00	_____ $6.00	_____ $2.00	_____
Turtleneck	_____ $12.00	_____ $5.00	_____ $2.00	_____
Dress				
Long-Sleeve	_____ $24.00	_____ $10.00	_____ $3.00	_____
Short-Sleeve	_____ $20.00	_____ $8.00	_____ $3.00	_____
Dresses				
Casual	_____ $28.00	_____ $15.00	_____ $3.00	_____
Dress	_____ $49.00	_____ $20.00	_____ $3.00	_____
Summer	_____ $24.00	_____ $12.00	_____ $3.00	_____
Wool	_____ $20.00	_____ $16.00	_____ $3.00	_____

See pages 11 & 12 for important information about properly valuing your donated items.

Women's Clothing

Description	High* Good Condition	Average* Fair Condition	Low* Poor Condition	Total
Exercise				
Jackets				
Fleece wHood	_____ $20.00	_____ $10.00	_____ $3.00	_____
Nylon wHood	_____ $18.00	_____ $8.00	_____ $3.00	_____
Nylon, Insulated wHood	_____ $20.00	_____ $9.00	_____ $3.00	_____
Leotards	_____ $8.00	_____ $4.00	_____ $2.00	_____
Pants				
Fleece	_10_ $12.00	_____ $6.00	_____ $3.00	120
Nylon	_____ $10.00	_____ $6.00	_____ $3.00	_____
Shirts				
Fleece, Long-Sleeve	_10_ $14.00	_____ $6.00	_____ $3.00	140
Fleece, Short-Sleeve	_____ $10.00	_____ $5.00	_____ $3.00	_____
Nylon, Long-Sleeve wZipper	_____ $10.00	_____ $5.00	_____ $3.00	_____
Shorts				
Fleece	_____ $12.00	_____ $5.00	_____ $3.00	_____
Nylon	_____ $12.00	_____ $5.00	_____ $3.00	_____
Formals				
Long	_____ $120.00	_____ $40.00	_____ $10.00	_____
Shorts	_____ $95.00	_____ $55.00	_____ $21.00	_____
Wedding Gown	_____ $250.00	_____ $108.00	_____ $30.00	_____
Maternity				
Casual Tops				
Long-Sleeve	_____ $12.00	_____ $7.00	_____ $3.00	_____
Short-Sleeve	_____ $11.00	_____ $6.00	_____ $3.00	_____
Dress Tops				
Long-Sleeve	_____ $19.00	_____ $9.00	_____ $3.00	_____
Short-Sleeve	_____ $14.00	_____ $8.00	_____ $3.00	_____
Dresses				
Casual	_____ $25.00	_____ $13.00	_____ $3.00	_____
Dress	_____ $35.00	_____ $18.00	_____ $3.00	_____
Skirts	_____ $12.00	_____ $8.00	_____ $3.00	_____

See pages 11 & 12 for important information about properly valuing your donated items.

Women's Clothing

Description	High* Good Condition	Average* Fair Condition	Low* Poor Condition	Total
Slacks				
Casual	_____ $15.00	_____ $8.00	_____ $3.00	_____
Dress	_____ $25.00	_____ $9.00	_____ $3.00	_____
Jumpers	_____ $18.00	_____ $11.00	_____ $3.00	_____
Suits				
Skirt and Jacket	_____ $40.00	_____ $20.00	_____ $3.00	_____
Slacks and Jacket	_____ $40.00	_____ $20.00	_____ $3.00	_____
Outerwear				
Casual Jackets				
Cloth	_____ $24.00	_____ $12.00	_____ $3.00	_____
Nylon	_____ $20.00	_____ $10.00	_____ $3.00	_____
Casual Winter Coats				
Ski	_____ $40.00	_____ $20.00	_____ $6.00	_____
Other	_____ $30.00	_____ $16.00	_____ $6.00	_____
Dress Jackets				
Cloth	_____ $45.00	_____ $15.00	_____ $5.00	_____
Wool	_____ $50.00	_____ $20.00	_____ $5.00	_____
Dress Winter Coats				
All Weather	_____ $39.00	_____ $24.00	_____ $5.00	_____
Wool Cape	_____ $50.00	_____ $28.00	_____ $5.00	_____
Wool Coat	_____ $50.00	_____ $28.00	_____ $5.00	_____
Other	_____ $30.00	_____ $20.00	_____ $8.00	_____
Leather Coats				
Casual	_____ $80.00	_____ $40.00	_____ $15.00	_____
Dress	_____ $80.00	_____ $40.00	_____ $15.00	_____
Rainwear				
Coat	_____ $35.00	_____ $18.00	_____ $3.00	_____
Shoes and Boots				
Boot, Snow	_____ $18.00	_____ $8.00	_____ $4.00	_____
Casual				
Boot, Leather	1 $50.00	_____ $12.00	_____ $4.00	50
Boot, Other	_____ $28.00	_____ $10.00	_____ $4.00	_____
Shoe, Slip-On	_____ $15.00	_____ $6.00	_____ $3.00	_____
Shoe, wLaces	2 $16.00	_____ $7.00	_____ $3.00	32

See pages 11 & 12 for important information about properly valuing your donated items.

Women's Clothing

Description	High* Good Condition	Average* Fair Condition	Low* Poor Condition	Total
Dress				
Boot, Leather	_____ $50.00	_____ $12.00	_____ $4.00	_____
Boot, Other	_____ $29.00	_____ $10.00	_____ $4.00	_____
Pumps, Leather	_____ $16.00	_____ $8.00	_____ $3.00	_____
Shoe, Leather	_____ $25.00	_____ $10.00	_____ $3.00	_____
Shoe, Other	_____ $18.00	_____ $8.00	_____ $3.00	_____
Sandals				
Leather	1 $23.00	_____ $8.00	_____ $3.00	23
Moccasins	_____ $15.00	_____ $7.00	_____ $3.00	
Slippers	2 $6.00	_____ $4.00	_____ $1.00	12
Sport				
Sneaker, Cloth	_____ $16.00	_____ $6.00	_____ $3.00	_____
Sneaker, Leather	_____ $20.00	_____ $7.00	_____ $2.00	_____
Tap	_____ $10.00	_____ $6.00	_____ $3.00	_____
Water Socks	_____ $6.00	_____ $4.00	_____ $2.00	_____
Skirts				
Jumpers				
Casual	_____ $24.00	_____ $12.00	_____ $3.00	_____
Dress	_____ $24.00	_____ $12.00	_____ $3.00	_____
Mini				
Denim	_____ $17.00	_____ $7.00	_____ $3.00	_____
Leather	_____ $29.00	_____ $12.00	_____ $3.00	_____
Other	_____ $12.00	_____ $6.00	_____ $3.00	_____
Regular				
Corduroy	_____ $12.00	_____ $7.00	_____ $3.00	_____
Denim	_____ $15.00	_____ $8.00	_____ $3.00	_____
Other	2 $16.00	3 $7.00	_____ $3.00	53

See pages 11 & 12 for important information about properly valuing your donated items.

Women's Clothing

Description	High* Good Condition	Average* Fair Condition	Low* Poor Condition	Total
Slacks and Pants				
Casual				
Corduroy	_____ $16.00	_____ $8.00	_____ $3.00	_____
Denim	_____ $18.00	_____ $8.00	_____ $3.00	_____
Other	_____ $15.00	_____ $7.00	_____ $3.00	_____
Dress	_____ $24.00	_____ $10.00	_____ $3.00	_____
Sleepwear				
Night Shirt	_____ $10.00	_____ $6.00	_____ $2.00	_____
Nightgown	_____ $16.00	_____ $7.00	_____ $2.00	_____
Pajamas				
Matching Set	_____ $15.00	_____ $8.00	_____ $2.00	_____
Robe	_____ $21.00	_____ $10.00	_____ $3.00	_____
Teddies	_____ $10.00	_____ $5.00	_____ $2.00	_____
Suits				
Custom Tailored				
Skirt and Jacket	_____ $79.00	_____ $25.00	_____ $6.00	_____
Slacks and Jacket	_____ $79.00	_____ $25.00	_____ $6.00	_____
Jacket	_____ $35.00	_____ $18.00	_____ $3.00	_____
Skirt	_____ $25.00	_____ $10.00	_____ $3.00	_____
Skirt and Jacket	_____ $60.00	_____ $22.00	_____ $6.00	_____
Slacks	_____ $20.00	_____ $10.00	_____ $3.00	_____
Slacks and Jacket	_____ $60.00	_____ $21.00	_____ $6.00	_____
Summerwear				
Shorts				
Denim	_____ $12.00	_____ $6.00	_____ $3.00	_____
Other	_____ $10.00	_____ $6.00	_____ $1.00	_____
Swimsuits				
Maternity	_____ $15.00	_____ $8.00	_____ $3.00	_____
One-Piece	_____ $14.00	_____ $9.00	_____ $3.00	_____
Two Piece	_____ $15.00	_____ $8.00	_____ $3.00	_____
Tops				
Tank	_____ $8.00	_____ $4.00	_____ $1.00	_____

See pages 11 & 12 for important information about properly valuing your donated items.

Women's Clothing

Description	High* Good Condition	Average* Fair Condition	Low* Poor Condition	Total
T-Shirt	_____ $14.00	_____ $4.00	_____ $1.00	_____
Other	_____ $8.00	_____ $6.00	_____ $3.00	_____
Sweaters				
Casual				
Cardigan	_____ $18.00	_____ $10.00	_____ $3.00	_____
Pullover Long-Sleeve	_____ $24.00	_____ $9.00	_____ $3.00	_____
Turtleneck	_____ $15.00	_____ $6.00	_____ $3.00	_____
Vest	_____ $15.00	_____ $7.00	_____ $1.00	_____
Dress				
Cardigan	_____ $18.00	_____ $10.00	_____ $3.00	_____
Pullover Long-Sleeve	_____ $24.00	_____ $9.00	_____ $3.00	_____
Turtleneck	_____ $15.00	_____ $6.00	_____ $3.00	_____
Vest	_____ $15.00	_____ $7.00	_____ $1.00	_____
V-Neck	_____ $16.00	_____ $8.00	_____ $3.00	_____
Undergarments				
Bras				
Regular	_____ $6.00	_____ $4.00	_____ $1.00	_____
Sport	_____ $6.00	_____ $3.00	_____ $1.00	_____
Girdle	_____ $5.00	_____ $3.00	_____ $1.00	_____
Panties				
Bikini	2 $3.00	3 $1.00	_____ $0.50	9
Regular	_____ $5.00	_____ $2.00	_____ $1.00	_____
Slips				
Camisole	_____ $8.00	_____ $4.00	_____ $1.00	_____
Full	_____ $8.00	_____ $5.00	_____ $1.00	_____
Half	_____ $6.00	_____ $3.00	_____ $1.00	_____
Socks (Pair)				
Dress	_____ $2.00	_____ $1.00	_____ $0.50	_____
Other	2 $2.00	5 $1.00	_____ $0.50	9
Tights	_____ $4.00	_____ $2.00	_____ $1.00	_____

TOTAL WOMEN'S CLOTHING	**$ 448**

See pages 11 & 12 for important information about properly valuing your donated items.

Men's Clothing

Description	High* Good Condition	Average* Fair Condition	Low* Poor Condition	Total
Accessories				
Belts				
Casual, Leather	_____ $9.00	_____ $3.00	_____ $1.00	_____
Cloth	_____ $5.00	_____ $3.00	_____ $1.00	_____
Dress, Leather	_____ $15.00	_____ $5.00	_____ $1.00	_____
Caps				
Stocking	_____ $5.00	_____ $3.00	_____ $1.00	_____
Summer	_____ $8.00	_____ $3.00	_____ $1.00	_____
Sun Visor	_____ $5.00	_____ $2.00	_____ $1.00	_____
Winter	_____ $12.00	_____ $3.00	_____ $1.00	_____
Handkerchiefs	_____ $2.00	_____ $1.00	_____ $0.50	_____
Hats				
Cowboy	_____ $35.00	_____ $10.00	_____ $2.00	_____
Dress	_____ $14.00	_____ $7.00	_____ $2.00	_____
Scarves				
Dress	_____ $10.00	_____ $3.00	_____ $1.00	_____
Other	_____ $6.00	_____ $3.00	_____ $1.00	_____
Suspenders				
Button-On	_____ $6.00	_____ $3.00	_____ $1.00	_____
Clip-On	_____ $7.00	_____ $3.00	_____ $1.00	_____
Ties				
Clip-On	_____ $4.00	_____ $2.00	_____ $1.00	_____
Silk	_____ $9.00	_____ $5.00	_____ $1.00	_____
Other	_____ $6.00	_____ $3.00	_____ $1.00	_____
Exercise				
Jackets				
Fleece Insulated wHood	_____ $19.00	_____ $10.00	_____ $3.00	_____
Fleece wHood	_____ $19.00	_____ $8.00	_____ $3.00	_____
Nylon	_____ $18.00	_____ $7.00	_____ $3.00	_____
Jock	_____ $6.00	_____ $2.00	_____ $1.00	_____

See pages 11 & 12 for important information about properly valuing your donated items.

Men's Clothing

Description	High* Good Condition	Average* Fair Condition	Low* Poor Condition	Total
Pants				
Fleece	_____ $10.00	_____ $6.00	_____ $2.00	_____
Nylon	_____ $10.00	_____ $6.00	_____ $2.00	_____
Shirts				
Nylon Long-Sleeve	_____ $12.00	_____ $6.00	_____ $3.00	_____
Sweatshirt Long-Sleeve	_____ $15.00	_____ $6.00	_____ $3.00	_____
Sweatshirt Short-Sleeve	_____ $11.00	_____ $6.00	_____ $3.00	_____
Shorts				
Fleece	_____ $8.00	_____ $5.00	_____ $2.00	_____
Nylon	_____ $8.00	_____ $5.00	_____ $2.00	_____
Suits (Matching Pants and Top)				
Fleece	_____ $24.00	_____ $12.00	_____ $4.00	_____
Nylon	_____ $29.00	_____ $12.00	_____ $4.00	_____
Outerwear				
Casual Jackets				
Cloth	_____ $20.00	_____ $9.00	_____ $4.00	_____
Nylon	_____ $16.00	_____ $8.00	_____ $3.00	_____
Casual Winter Coats				
Ski	_____ $51.00	_____ $20.00	_____ $6.00	_____
Other	_____ $27.00	_____ $16.00	_____ $6.00	_____
Coveralls	_____ $20.00	_____ $11.00	_____ $5.00	_____
Dress Jackets				
Wool	_____ $35.00	_____ $19.00	_____ $6.00	_____
Dress Winter Coats				
All Weather	_____ $60.00	_____ $25.00	_____ $6.00	_____
Wool	_____ $75.00	_____ $30.00	_____ $6.00	_____
Other	_____ $51.00	_____ $18.00	_____ $6.00	_____
Gloves				
Dress	_____ $7.00	_____ $4.00	_____ $1.00	_____
Leather Coats				
Casual	_____ $80.00	_____ $45.00	_____ $10.00	_____
Dress	_____ $80.00	_____ $45.00	_____ $10.00	_____

See pages 11 & 12 for important information about properly valuing your donated items.

Men's Clothing

Description	High* Good Condition	Average* Fair Condition	Low* Poor Condition	Total
Rainwear				
Coat	_____ $39.00	_____ $12.00	_____ $3.00	_____
Ski Bibs	_____ $25.00	_____ $11.00	_____ $4.00	_____
Snow Mobile Outfit	_____ $29.00	_____ $13.00	_____ $5.00	_____
Vests				
Suede	_____ $16.00	_____ $10.00	_____ $2.00	_____
Winter	_____ $16.00	_____ $8.00	_____ $2.00	_____
Shirts				
Casual				
Long-Sleeve	5 $18.00	_____ $8.00	_____ $2.00	90
Short-Sleeve	2 $17.00	_____ $6.00	_____ $2.00	34
Turtleneck	_____ $12.00	_____ $5.00	_____ $2.00	_____
Dress				
Long-Sleeve	5 $18.00	_____ $8.00	_____ $2.00	90
Short-Sleeve	_____ $16.00	_____ $7.00	_____ $2.00	_____
Sport				
Pullover Long-Sleeve	_____ $18.00	_____ $8.00	_____ $2.00	_____
Pullover Short-Sleeve	_____ $16.00	_____ $6.00	_____ $2.00	_____
Work				
Long-Sleeve	_____ $16.00	_____ $5.00	_____ $2.00	_____
Short-Sleeve	_____ $15.00	_____ $5.00	_____ $2.00	_____
Shoes and Boots				
Boots, Snow	_____ $15.00	_____ $8.00	_____ $3.00	_____
Casual				
Boot, Slip-On	_____ $20.00	_____ $8.00	_____ $4.00	_____
Boot, Western	_____ $51.00	_____ $13.00	_____ $4.00	_____
Shoe, Slip-On	_____ $21.00	_____ $8.00	_____ $3.00	_____
Shoe, wLaces	_____ $24.00	_____ $8.00	_____ $3.00	_____
Dress				
Boot, Leather Slip-On	_____ $39.00	_____ $10.00	_____ $4.00	_____
Shoe, Leather Slip-On	_____ $19.00	_____ $8.00	_____ $3.00	_____
Shoe, Leather wLaces	_____ $25.00	_____ $10.00	_____ $3.00	_____

See pages 11 & 12 for important information about properly valuing your donated items.

Men's Clothing

Description	High* Good Condition	Average* Fair Condition	Low* Poor Condition	Total
Slippers	_____ $8.00	_____ $4.00	_____ $1.00	_____
Sport				
Boot, Hiking wLaces	_____ $20.00	_____ $9.00	_____ $4.00	_____
Boot, Hunting wLaces	_____ $15.00	_____ $9.00	_____ $4.00	_____
Football or Softball	_____ $9.00	_____ $8.00	_____ $7.00	_____
Sneaker, Leather	_____ $30.00	_____ $9.00	_____ $3.00	_____
Slacks and Pants				
Casual				
Corduroy	_1_ $17.00	_____ $8.00	_____ $3.00	17
Denim	_3_ $19.00	_____ $9.00	_____ $3.00	57
Other	_____ $14.00	_____ $7.00	_____ $2.00	_____
Dress	_6_ $17.00	_____ $8.00	_____ $3.00	102
Sleepwear				
Pajamas				
Matching Set	_____ $12.00	_____ $7.00	_____ $2.00	4
Robe	_____ $15.00	_____ $9.00	_____ $3.00	_____
Suits				
Casual				
Sports Coat	_____ $46.00	_____ $15.00	_____ $5.00	_____
Custom Tailored				
Two Piece	_____ $89.00	_____ $35.00	_____ $10.00	_____
Dress				
Coat	_____ $75.00	_____ $15.00	_____ $5.00	_____
Slacks	_____ $19.00	_____ $9.00	_____ $3.00	_____
Two Piece	_____ $110.00	_____ $30.00	_____ $10.00	_____
Vest	_____ $10.00	_____ $5.00	_____ $2.00	_____
Summerwear				
Shirts				
Tank	_____ $6.00	_____ $4.00	_____ $1.00	_____
T-Shirt	_2_ $8.00	_____ $4.00	_____ $1.00	16
Shorts				
Denim	_____ $12.00	_____ $6.00	_____ $2.00	_____
Other	_____ $10.00	_3_ $5.00	_____ $1.00	15

See pages 11 & 12 for important information about properly valuing your donated items.

Men's Clothing

Description	High* Good Condition	Average* Fair Condition	Low* Poor Condition	Total
Swimwear	_____ $10.00	_____ $6.00	_____ $3.00	_____
Sweaters				
Casual				
Cardigan	_____ $20.00	_____ $8.00	_____ $3.00	_____
Pullover Long-Sleeve	_____ $20.00	_____ $9.00	_____ $3.00	_____
Turtleneck	_____ $15.00	_____ $6.00	_____ $3.00	_____
Vest	_____ $15.00	_____ $6.00	_____ $2.00	_____
V-Neck	_____ $16.00	_____ $8.00	_____ $3.00	_____
Dress				
Cardigan	_____ $20.00	_____ $8.00	_____ $3.00	_____
Pullover Long-Sleeve	_____ $20.00	_____ $9.00	_____ $3.00	_____
Turtleneck	_____ $15.00	_____ $6.00	_____ $3.00	_____
Vest	_____ $15.00	_____ $6.00	_____ $2.00	_____
V-Neck	_____ $16.00	_____ $8.00	_____ $3.00	_____
Undergarments				
Pants				
Insulated	_____ $6.00	_____ $3.00	_____ $1.00	_____
Shirts				
Insulated Long-Sleeve	_____ $7.00	_____ $3.00	_____ $1.00	_____
T-Shirt	_____ $5.00	_____ $2.00	_____ $1.00	_____
Socks (Pair)				
Dress	_____ $3.00	_____ $1.00	_____ $0.50	_____
Other	_____ $2.00	_____ $1.00	_____ $0.50	_____
Underwear				
Bikini	_____ $3.00	_____ $1.00	_____ $0.50	_____
Boxer	_____ $5.00	_____ $2.00	_____ $1.00	_____
Regular	_5_ $5.00	_____ $1.00	_____ $0.50	_25_
TOTAL MEN'S CLOTHING			$ _460_	

Girl's Clothing

Description	High* Good Condition	Average* Fair Condition	Low* Poor Condition	Total
Accessories				
Belts				
Leather	____ $5.00	____ $2.00	____ $1.00	_____
Other	____ $5.00	____ $2.00	____ $1.00	_____
Caps				
Biking	____ $5.00	____ $2.00	____ $1.00	_____
Stocking	____ $4.00	____ $1.00	____ $0.50	_____
Hats				
Dress	____ $10.00	____ $4.00	____ $1.00	_____
Summer	____ $10.00	____ $3.00	____ $1.00	_____
Purses	____ $7.00	____ $3.00	____ $1.00	_____
Scarves	____ $4.00	____ $2.00	____ $1.00	_____
Blouses and Shirts				
Casual				
Long-Sleeve	____ $9.00	____ $5.00	____ $2.00	_____
Short-Sleeve	____ $8.00	____ $4.00	____ $1.00	_____
Turtleneck	____ $7.00	____ $3.00	____ $1.00	_____
Dress				
Long-Sleeve	____ $10.00	____ $6.00	____ $2.00	_____
Short-Sleeve	____ $9.00	____ $5.00	____ $2.00	_____
Dresses				
Casual	____ $15.00	____ $7.00	____ $2.00	_____
Dress	____ $24.00	____ $12.00	____ $2.00	_____
Summer	____ $14.00	____ $8.00	____ $2.00	_____
Exercise				
Jackets				
Fleece, Insulated wHood	____ $18.00	____ $7.00	____ $2.00	_____
Fleece, wHood	____ $16.00	____ $6.00	____ $2.00	_____
Leotards	____ $8.00	____ $3.00	____ $1.00	_____
Pants				
Fleece	____ $9.00	____ $4.00	____ $2.00	_____
Nylon	____ $8.00	____ $4.00	____ $1.00	_____

See pages 11 & 12 for important information about properly valuing your donated items.

Girl's Clothing

Description	High* Good Condition	Average* Fair Condition	Low* Poor Condition	Total
Shirts				
Sweatshirt, Long-Sleeve	_____ $10.00	_____ $4.00	_____ $2.00	_____
Sweatshirt, Short-Sleeve	_____ $8.00	_____ $3.00	_____ $2.00	_____
Shorts				
Fleece	_____ $7.00	_____ $3.00	_____ $1.00	_____
Nylon	_____ $5.00	_____ $3.00	_____ $1.00	_____
Suits (Matching Pants and Top)				
Fleece	_____ $15.00	_____ $8.00	_____ $3.00	_____
Nylon	_____ $12.00	_____ $7.00	_____ $3.00	_____
Outerwear				
Casual Jackets				
Cloth	_____ $19.00	_____ $8.00	_____ $2.00	_____
Other	_____ $15.00	_____ $7.00	_____ $2.00	_____
Casual Winter Coats				
Ski	_____ $25.00	_____ $12.00	_____ $3.00	_____
Other	_____ $17.00	_____ $10.00	_____ $3.00	_____
Dress Jackets	_____ $40.00	_____ $10.00	_____ $2.00	_____
Dress Winter Coats				
All Weather	_____ $40.00	_____ $12.00	_____ $2.00	_____
Ear Muffs	_____ $5.00	_____ $2.00	_____ $1.00	_____
Rainwear				
Coat	_____ $15.00	_____ $7.00	_____ $2.00	_____
Ski Bibs	_____ $19.00	_____ $8.00	_____ $3.00	_____
Shoes and Boots				
Boot, Snow	_____ $10.00	_____ $6.00	_____ $3.00	_____
Casual				
Shoe, Leather Slip-On	_____ $10.00	_____ $5.00	_____ $2.00	_____
Shoe, Leather wLaces	_____ $10.00	_____ $5.00	_____ $2.00	_____
Dress				
Shoe, Leather Slip-On	_____ $11.00	_____ $5.00	_____ $2.00	_____
Shoe, Leather wLaces	_____ $11.00	_____ $5.00	_____ $2.00	_____
Sandals	_____ $8.00	_____ $4.00	_____ $1.00	_____

See pages 11 & 12 for important information about properly valuing your donated items.

Girl's Clothing

Description	High* Good Condition	Average* Fair Condition	Low* Poor Condition	Total
Slippers	_____ $6.00	_____ $2.00	_____ $1.00	_____
Sport				
Sneaker, Cloth	_____ $10.00	_____ $5.00	_____ $1.00	_____
Sneaker, Leather	_____ $12.00	_____ $5.00	_____ $2.00	_____
Skirts				
Jumpers				
Casual	_____ $14.00	_____ $6.00	_____ $2.00	_____
Dress	_____ $14.00	_____ $6.00	_____ $2.00	_____
Regular				
Denim	_____ $9.00	_____ $5.00	_____ $2.00	_____
Other	_____ $8.00	_____ $4.00	_____ $2.00	_____
Slacks and Pants				
Casual				
Corduroy	_____ $9.00	_____ $5.00	_____ $2.00	_____
Denim	_____ $10.00	_____ $6.00	_____ $2.00	_____
Other	_____ $8.00	_____ $4.00	_____ $2.00	_____
Dress	_____ $10.00	_____ $5.00	_____ $2.00	_____
Summerwear				
Shorts				
Denim	_____ $9.00	_____ $5.00	_____ $2.00	_____
Other	_____ $8.00	_____ $4.00	_____ $1.00	_____
Swimwear				
One-Piece	_____ $10.00	_____ $5.00	_____ $2.00	_____
Two Piece	_____ $10.00	_____ $5.00	_____ $2.00	_____
Tops				
Tank	_____ $7.00	_____ $4.00	_____ $2.00	_____
T-Shirt	_____ $7.00	_____ $3.00	_____ $1.00	_____
Other	_____ $7.00	_____ $4.00	_____ $1.00	_____
Sweaters				
Casual				
Cardigan	_____ $12.00	_____ $5.00	_____ $2.00	_____
Pullover, Long-Sleeve	_____ $12.00	_____ $6.00	_____ $2.00	_____

See pages 11 & 12 for important information about properly valuing your donated items.

Girl's Clothing

Description	High* Good Condition	Average* Fair Condition	Low* Poor Condition	Total
Vest	_____ $9.00	_____ $4.00	_____ $1.00	_____
V-Neck	_____ $9.00	_____ $4.00	_____ $2.00	_____
Dress				
Cardigan	_____ $12.00	_____ $5.00	_____ $2.00	_____
Pullover, Long-Sleeve	_____ $12.00	_____ $6.00	_____ $2.00	_____
Vest	_____ $9.00	_____ $4.00	_____ $1.00	_____
V-Neck	_____ $9.00	_____ $4.00	_____ $2.00	_____
Undergarments				
Night Shirt	_____ $6.00	_____ $4.00	_____ $1.00	_____
Nightgown	_____ $8.00	_____ $4.00	_____ $1.00	_____
Pajamas	_____ $8.00	_____ $4.00	_____ $1.00	_____
Panties				
Bikini	_____ $1.50	_____ $1.00	_____ $0.50	_____
Regular	_____ $2.00	_____ $1.00	_____ $0.50	_____
Robe	_____ $12.00	_____ $5.00	_____ $2.00	_____
Slips				
Camisole	_____ $4.00	_____ $2.00	_____ $1.00	_____
Full	_____ $6.00	_____ $3.00	_____ $1.00	_____
Half	_____ $4.00	_____ $2.00	_____ $1.00	_____
Socks (Pair)				
Dress	_____ $2.00	_____ $1.00	_____ $0.50	_____
Other	_____ $2.00	_____ $1.00	_____ $0.50	_____
TOTAL GIRL'S CLOTHING				**$**

See pages 11 & 12 for important information about properly valuing your donated items.

Boy's Clothing

Description	High* Good Condition	Average* Fair Condition	Low* Poor Condition	Total
Accessories				
Belts				
Dress, Leather	_____ $8.00	_____ $3.00	_____ $1.00	_____
Other	_____ $5.00	_____ $2.00	_____ $1.00	_____
Caps				
Baseball	_____ $5.00	_____ $2.00	_____ $1.00	_____
Stocking	_____ $5.00	_____ $2.00	_____ $1.00	_____
Sun Visor	_____ $3.00	_____ $1.00	_____ $0.50	_____
Scarves				
Dress	_____ $5.00	_____ $2.00	_____ $1.00	_____
Winter	_____ $6.00	_____ $2.00	_____ $1.00	_____
Suspenders				
Button Clip-On	_____ $4.00	_____ $2.00	_____ $1.00	_____
Ties	_____ $5.00	_____ $2.00	_____ $1.00	_____
Exercise				
Jackets				
Fleece, Insulated wHood	_____ $14.00	_____ $6.00	_____ $2.00	_____
Fleece, wHood	_____ $18.00	_____ $6.00	_____ $2.00	_____
Pants				
Fleece	_____ $10.00	_____ $5.00	_____ $2.00	_____
Nylon	_____ $8.00	_____ $4.00	_____ $2.00	_____
Shirts				
Fleece, Long-Sleeve	_____ $12.00	_____ $5.00	_____ $2.00	_____
Fleece, Short-Sleeve	_____ $8.00	_____ $4.00	_____ $2.00	_____
Shorts				
Fleece	_____ $6.00	_____ $4.00	_____ $1.00	_____
Nylon	_____ $6.00	_____ $3.00	_____ $1.00	_____
Suits (Matching Pants and Top)				
Fleece	_____ $15.00	_____ $8.00	_____ $2.00	_____
Nylon	_____ $14.00	_____ $8.00	_____ $3.00	_____

See pages 11 & 12 for important information about properly valuing your donated items.

Boy's Clothing

Description	High* Good Condition	Average* Fair Condition	Low* Poor Condition	Total
Outerwear				
Casual Jackets				
Cloth	_____ $16.00	_____ $8.00	_____ $2.00	_____
Denim	_____ $19.00	_____ $8.00	_____ $2.00	_____
Casual Winter Coats				
Ski	_____ $25.00	_____ $12.00	_____ $2.00	_____
Dress Winter Coats				
All Weather	_____ $30.00	_____ $14.00	_____ $2.00	_____
Mittens and Gloves	_____ $5.00	_____ $2.00	_____ $1.00	_____
Ski Pants	_____ $15.00	_____ $6.00	_____ $2.00	_____
Vests				
Winter	_____ $14.00	_____ $6.00	_____ $2.00	_____
Shirts				
Casual				
Flannel, Long-Sleeve	_____ $8.00	_____ $4.00	_____ $2.00	_____
Long-Sleeve	_____ $9.00	_____ $5.00	_____ $2.00	_____
Short-Sleeve	_____ $7.00	_____ $4.00	_____ $2.00	_____
Turtleneck	_____ $7.00	_____ $4.00	_____ $1.00	_____
Dress				
Long-Sleeve	_____ $10.00	_____ $5.00	_____ $2.00	_____
Short-Sleeve	_____ $9.00	_____ $4.00	_____ $2.00	_____
Sport				
Pullover, Long-Sleeve	_____ $9.00	_____ $5.00	_____ $2.00	_____
Pullover, Short-Sleeve	_____ $8.00	_____ $4.00	_____ $1.00	_____
Shoes and Boots				
Boots, Snow	_____ $12.00	_____ $7.00	_____ $3.00	_____
Casual				
Boots, Western	_____ $15.00	_____ $8.00	_____ $3.00	_____
Shoe, Slip-On	_____ $12.00	_____ $5.00	_____ $1.00	_____
Shoe, wLaces	_____ $12.00	_____ $6.00	_____ $1.00	_____
Dress				
Shoe, Leather Slip-On	_____ $14.00	_____ $6.00	_____ $1.00	_____
Shoe, Leather wLaces	_____ $15.00	_____ $6.00	_____ $1.00	_____

See pages 11 & 12 for important information about properly valuing your donated items.

Boy's Clothing

Description	High* Good Condition	Average* Fair Condition	Low* Poor Condition	Total
Slippers	_____ $6.00	_____ $3.00	_____ $1.00	_____
Sport				
Sneaker, Cloth	_____ $9.00	_____ $5.00	_____ $1.00	_____
Sneaker, Leather	_____ $14.00	_____ $8.00	_____ $1.00	_____
Slacks and Pants				
Casual				
Corduroy	_____ $10.00	_____ $5.00	_____ $2.00	_____
Denim	_____ $12.00	_____ $6.00	_____ $2.00	_____
Other	_____ $10.00	_____ $5.00	_____ $2.00	_____
Dress	_____ $13.00	_____ $8.00	_____ $2.00	_____
Sleepwear				
Pajamas				
Set (Pants and Shirt)	_____ $8.00	_____ $4.00	_____ $2.00	_____
Robe	_____ $11.00	_____ $5.00	_____ $2.00	_____
Suits				
Casual				
Sport Coat	_____ $22.00	_____ $10.00	_____ $2.00	_____
Dress				
Coat	_____ $20.00	_____ $10.00	_____ $2.00	_____
Slacks	_____ $12.00	_____ $7.00	_____ $2.00	_____
Two Piece	_____ $28.00	_____ $15.00	_____ $4.00	_____
Summerwear				
Shirts				
Tank	_____ $6.00	_____ $3.00	_____ $1.00	_____
T-Shirt	_____ $6.00	_____ $3.00	_____ $1.00	_____
Shorts				
Denim	_____ $9.00	_____ $5.00	_____ $2.00	_____
Other	_____ $7.00	_____ $4.00	_____ $1.00	_____
Swimwear	_____ $8.00	_____ $4.00	_____ $2.00	_____

See pages 11 & 12 for important information about properly valuing your donated items.

Boy's Clothing

Description	High* Good Condition	Average* Fair Condition	Low* Poor Condition	Total
Sweaters				
Casual				
Cardigan	_____ $12.00	_____ $6.00	_____ $2.00	_____
Pullover, Long-Sleeve	_____ $15.00	_____ $6.00	_____ $2.00	_____
Vest	_____ $9.00	_____ $4.00	_____ $1.00	_____
V-Neck	_____ $10.00	_____ $5.00	_____ $2.00	_____
Dress				
Cardigan	_____ $12.00	_____ $6.00	_____ $2.00	_____
Pullover, Long-Sleeve	_____ $15.00	_____ $6.00	_____ $2.00	_____
Vest	_____ $9.00	_____ $4.00	_____ $1.00	_____
V-Neck	_____ $10.00	_____ $5.00	_____ $2.00	_____
Undergarments				
Pants				
Insulated	_____ $5.00	_____ $3.00	_____ $1.00	_____
Shirts				
Long-Sleeve, Insulated	_____ $5.00	_____ $3.00	_____ $1.00	_____
T-Shirt	_____ $4.00	_____ $2.00	_____ $1.00	_____
Socks (Pair)				
Dress	_____ $3.00	_____ $1.00	_____ $0.50	_____
Other	_____ $2.00	_____ $1.00	_____ $0.50	_____
Underwear				
Regular	_____ $3.00	_____ $1.00	_____ $0.50	_____
TOTAL BOY'S CLOTHING				**$**

See pages 11 & 12 for important information about properly valuing your donated items.

Toddler's Clothing

Description	High* Good Condition	Average* Fair Condition	Low* Poor Condition	Total
Dresses				
Casual	_____ $16.00	_____ $8.00	_____ $3.00	_____
Dress	_____ $21.00	_____ $8.00	_____ $4.00	_____
Exercise				
Jackets				
Fleece, wHood	_____ $15.00	_____ $5.00	_____ $1.00	_____
Pants				
Fleece	_____ $8.00	_____ $4.00	_____ $1.00	_____
Nylon	_____ $6.00	_____ $3.00	_____ $1.00	_____
Shirts				
Nylon	_____ $7.00	_____ $3.00	_____ $1.00	_____
Sweatshirt	_____ $8.00	_____ $3.00	_____ $1.00	_____
Suits (Matching Pants and Top)				
Fleece	_____ $15.00	_____ $7.00	_____ $2.00	_____
Nylon	_____ $12.00	_____ $6.00	_____ $2.00	_____
Outerwear				
Bib Overalls				
Corduroy	_____ $10.00	_____ $6.00	_____ $1.00	_____
Denim	_____ $12.00	_____ $6.00	_____ $1.00	_____
Other	_____ $9.00	_____ $5.00	_____ $1.00	_____
Cap	_____ $5.00	_____ $2.00	_____ $1.00	_____
Gloves	_____ $4.00	_____ $2.00	_____ $1.00	_____
Jackets				
Casual	_____ $18.00	_____ $7.00	_____ $2.00	_____
Dress	_____ $25.00	_____ $8.00	_____ $4.00	_____
Raincoat	_____ $12.00	_____ $6.00	_____ $1.00	_____
Snowsuit	_____ $20.00	_____ $12.00	_____ $3.00	_____
Sweaters	_____ $12.00	_____ $5.00	_____ $1.00	_____
Winter Coats				
Casual	_____ $30.00	_____ $10.00	_____ $4.00	_____
Dress	_____ $25.00	_____ $12.00	_____ $6.00	_____

See pages 11 & 12 for important information about properly valuing your donated items.

Toddler's Clothing

Description	High* Good Condition	Average* Fair Condition	Low* Poor Condition	Total
Pants				
Denim	_____ $10.00	_____ $5.00	_____ $1.00	_____
Other	_____ $9.00	_____ $4.00	_____ $1.00	_____
Shirts and Blouses				
Long-Sleeve	_____ $8.00	_____ $5.00	_____ $1.00	_____
Short-Sleeve	_____ $7.00	_____ $4.00	_____ $1.00	_____
Turtleneck	_____ $7.00	_____ $3.00	_____ $1.00	_____
Shoes and Boots				
Boots, Leather	_____ $20.00	_____ $6.00	_____ $3.00	_____
Boots, Snow	_____ $15.00	_____ $6.00	_____ $2.00	_____
Shoe, Leather	_____ $10.00	_____ $5.00	_____ $1.00	_____
Shoe, Other	_____ $8.00	_____ $4.00	_____ $1.00	_____
Slippers	_____ $5.00	_____ $2.00	_____ $1.00	_____
Sneaker, Leather	_____ $10.00	_____ $4.00	_____ $1.00	_____
Skirts				
Casual	_____ $10.00	_____ $5.00	_____ $3.00	_____
Sleepwear				
Pajamas				
Gown	_____ $6.00	_____ $3.00	_____ $1.00	_____
Matching Set	_____ $6.00	_____ $3.00	_____ $1.00	_____
Sleepers, wFeet	_____ $6.00	_____ $4.00	_____ $1.00	_____
Sleepers, woFeet	_____ $6.00	_____ $3.00	_____ $1.00	_____
Suits				
Dress	_____ $22.00	_____ $12.00	_____ $1.00	_____
Summerwear				
Shirts				
Tank	_____ $5.00	_____ $2.00	_____ $1.00	_____
T-Shirt	_____ $5.00	_____ $2.00	_____ $1.00	_____
Shorts				
Denim	_____ $8.00	_____ $3.00	_____ $1.00	_____
Other	_____ $6.00	_____ $2.00	_____ $1.00	_____

See pages 11 & 12 for important information about properly valuing your donated items.

Toddler's Clothing

Description	High* Good Condition	Average* Fair Condition	Low* Poor Condition	Total
Sweaters				
Cardigan	_____ $12.00	_____ $5.00	_____ $1.00	_____
Pullover, Long-Sleeve	_____ $9.00	_____ $4.00	_____ $1.00	_____
Vest	_____ $5.00	_____ $3.00	_____ $1.00	_____
Undergarments				
Panties	_____ $2.00	_____ $1.00	_____ $0.50	_____
Plastic Pants	_____ $1.50	_____ $1.00	_____ $0.50	_____
Socks (Pair)				
Dress	_____ $2.00	_____ $1.00	_____ $0.50	_____
Other	_____ $1.50	_____ $1.00	_____ $0.50	_____
Swimsuits	_____ $10.00	_____ $4.00	_____ $2.00	_____
Tights	_____ $3.00	_____ $1.00	_____ $0.50	_____
Underwear	_____ $1.00	_____ $0.50	_____ $0.50	_____
TOTAL TODDLER'S CLOTHING			$	

See pages 11 & 12 for important information about properly valuing your donated items.

Infant's Clothing

Description	High* Good Condition	Average* Fair Condition	Low* Poor Condition	Total
Bedding				
Afghan	_____ $15.00	_____ $5.00	_____ $2.00	_____
Blankets	_____ $10.00	_____ $4.00	_____ $1.00	_____
Pillow	_____ $5.00	_____ $2.00	_____ $1.00	_____
Quilt	_____ $20.00	_____ $7.00	_____ $2.00	_____
Receiving Blanket	_____ $5.00	_____ $3.00	_____ $1.00	_____
Sheets, Set	_____ $10.00	_____ $4.00	_____ $2.00	_____
Dresses				
Casual	_____ $14.00	_____ $6.00	_____ $1.00	
Dress	_____ $14.00	_____ $6.00	_____ $1.00	
Outerwear				
Caps	_____ $5.00	_____ $2.00	_____ $1.00	
Coats, Winter	_____ $18.00	_____ $9.00	_____ $3.00	
Gloves and Mittens	_____ $4.00	_____ $1.50	_____ $1.00	
Jacket	_____ $14.00	_____ $6.00	_____ $1.00	
Snowsuits	_____ $20.00	_____ $11.00	_____ $3.00	
Stocking Cap	_____ $4.00	_____ $1.00	_____ $0.50	
Pants				
Casual	_____ $8.00	_____ $3.00	_____ $1.00	
Shirts				
Long-Sleeve	_____ $6.00	_____ $3.00	_____ $1.00	
Short-Sleeve	_____ $5.00	_____ $2.00	_____ $1.00	
Tank	_____ $5.00	_____ $2.00	_____ $1.00	
T-Shirt	_____ $5.00	_____ $2.00	_____ $1.00	
Shoes and Boots				
Shoes	_____ $9.00	_____ $5.00	_____ $2.00	
Sleepwear				
Gowns	_____ $5.00	_____ $3.00	_____ $1.00	
Sleeper, w/Feet	_____ $6.00	_____ $4.00	_____ $1.00	
Sleeper, w/o Feet	_____ $6.00	_____ $3.00	_____ $1.00	

See pages 11 & 12 for important information about properly valuing your donated items.

Infant's Clothing

Description	High* Good Condition	Average* Fair Condition	Low* Poor Condition	Total
Summerwear				
Play Suits				
Casual	_____ $8.00	_____ $4.00	_____ $1.00	_____
Shorts				
Casual	_____ $6.00	_____ $3.00	_____ $1.00	_____
Swimwear	_____ $6.00	_____ $4.00	_____ $1.00	_____
Sweaters				
Cardigan	_____ $10.00	_____ $4.00	_____ $1.00	_____
Pullover, Long-Sleeve	_____ $9.00	_____ $4.00	_____ $1.00	_____
Undergarments				
Booties	_____ $3.00	_____ $1.00	_____ $0.50	_____
Socks (Pair)	_____ $2.00	_____ $1.00	_____ $0.50	_____
Tights	_____ $3.00	_____ $1.00	_____ $0.50	_____
TOTAL INFANT'S CLOTHING			$	

*See pages 11 & 12 for important information about properly valuing your donated items.

Women's Designer Clothing

Description	High* Good Condition	Average* Fair Condition	Low* Poor Condition	Total
Accessories				
Belts				
Leather	_____ $30.00	_____ $14.00	_____ $2.00	_____
Other	_____ $30.00	_____ $10.00	_____ $2.00	_____
Gloves				
Dress	_____ $14.00	_____ $6.00	_____ $2.00	_____
Leather	_____ $15.00	_____ $9.00	_____ $8.00	_____
Purses				
Dress	_____ $110.00	_____ $30.00	_____ $20.00	_____
Leather	_____ $99.00	_____ $45.00	_____ $28.00	_____
Other	_____ $49.00	_____ $24.00	_____ $18.00	_____
Scarves				
Dress	_____ $20.00	_____ $10.00	_____ $8.00	_____
Other	_____ $12.00	_____ $9.00	_____ $6.00	_____
Blouses and Shirts				
Casual				
Long-Sleeve	_____ $30.00	_____ $17.00	_____ $6.00	_____
Short-Sleeve	_____ $28.00	_____ $13.00	_____ $8.00	_____
Turtleneck	_____ $16.00	_____ $9.00	_____ $9.00	_____
Dress				
Long-Sleeve	_____ $40.00	_____ $18.00	_____ $8.00	_____
Short-Sleeve	_____ $40.00	_____ $17.00	_____ $10.00	_____
Dresses				
Casual	_____ $60.00	_____ $20.00	_____ $14.00	_____
Dress	_____ $165.00	_____ $48.00	_____ $28.00	_____
Summer	_____ $49.00	_____ $19.00	_____ $12.00	_____
Wool	_____ $55.00	_____ $25.00	_____ $15.00	_____
Exercise				
Jackets				
Fleece	_____ $19.00	_____ $12.00	_____ $10.00	_____
Nylon	_____ $19.00	_____ $10.00	_____ $6.00	_____

See pages 11 & 12 for important information about properly valuing your donated items.

Women's Designer Clothing

Description	High* Good Condition	Average* Fair Condition	Low* Poor Condition	Total
Pants				
Fleece	_____ $14.00	_____ $8.00	_____ $6.00	_____
Nylon	_____ $12.00	_____ $8.00	_____ $6.00	_____
Shirts				
Sweatshirt, Long-Sleeve	_____ $20.00	_____ $10.00	_____ $6.00	_____
Sweatshirt, Short-Sleeve	_____ $10.00	_____ $9.00	_____ $6.00	_____
Shorts				
Fleece	_____ $9.00	_____ $6.00	_____ $2.00	_____
Nylon	_____ $9.00	_____ $6.00	_____ $2.00	_____
Formals				
Long	_____ $200.00	_____ $85.00	_____ $40.00	_____
Short	_____ $100.00	_____ $60.00	_____ $20.00	_____
Wedding Gown	_____ $300.00	_____ $110.00	_____ $75.00	_____
Jumpers				
Casual	_____ $28.00	_____ $18.00	_____ $12.00	_____
Dress	_____ $28.00	_____ $18.00	_____ $12.00	_____
Outerwear				
Casual Jackets				
Cloth	_____ $30.00	_____ $18.00	_____ $15.00	_____
Nylon	_____ $18.00	_____ $10.00	_____ $6.00	_____
Casual Winter Coats				
Ski	_____ $40.00	_____ $22.00	_____ $12.00	_____
Other	_____ $36.00	_____ $18.00	_____ $12.00	_____
Dress Jackets				
Cloth	_____ $60.00	_____ $25.00	_____ $10.00	_____
Wool	_____ $65.00	_____ $27.00	_____ $10.00	_____
Dress Winter Coats				
All Weather	_____ $100.00	_____ $45.00	_____ $15.00	_____
Wool	_____ $120.00	_____ $60.00	_____ $19.00	_____
Other	_____ $69.00	_____ $25.00	_____ $15.00	_____
Leather Coats				
Casual	_____ $150.00	_____ $80.00	_____ $25.00	_____
Dress	_____ $150.00	_____ $80.00	_____ $25.00	_____

See pages 11 & 12 for important information about properly valuing your donated items.

Women's Designer Clothing

Description	High* Good Condition	Average* Fair Condition	Low* Poor Condition	Total
Shoes and Boots				
Casual				
Boots, Leather	_____ $44.00	_____ $25.00	_____ $10.00	_____
Shoes, Slip-on	_____ $28.00	_____ $16.00	_____ $10.00	_____
Shoes, wLaces	_____ $32.00	_____ $19.00	_____ $10.00	_____
Dress				
Boots, Leather	_____ $79.00	_____ $40.00	_____ $20.00	_____
Boots, Other	_____ $40.00	_____ $26.00	_____ $12.00	_____
Pumps, Leather	_____ $42.00	_____ $19.00	_____ $10.00	_____
Shoes, Leather	_____ $39.00	_____ $19.00	_____ $12.00	_____
Shoes, Other	_____ $20.00	_____ $10.00	_____ $9.00	_____
Miscellaneous				
Boots, Snow	_____ $15.00	_____ $10.00	_____ $9.00	_____
Sandals	_____ $20.00	_____ $10.00	_____ $3.00	_____
Sport				
Sneakers, Cloth	_____ $14.00	_____ $10.00	_____ $6.00	_____
Sneakers, Other	_____ $10.00	_____ $9.00	_____ $6.00	_____
Skirts				
Casual				
Corduroy	_____ $20.00	_____ $10.00	_____ $4.00	_____
Denim	_____ $19.00	_____ $10.00	_____ $4.00	_____
Other	_____ $20.00	_____ $12.00	_____ $9.00	_____
Mini				
Denim	_____ $20.00	_____ $11.00	_____ $6.00	_____
Leather	_____ $48.00	_____ $22.00	_____ $17.00	_____
Other	_____ $15.00	_____ $10.00	_____ $6.00	_____
Slacks and Pants				
Casual				
Corduroy	_____ $20.00	_____ $13.00	_____ $8.00	_____
Denim	_____ $19.00	_____ $11.00	_____ $7.00	_____
Other	_____ $24.00	_____ $12.00	_____ $10.00	_____
Dress	_____ $49.00	_____ $20.00	_____ $12.00	_____

See pages 11 & 12 for important information about properly valuing your donated items.

Women's Designer Clothing

Description	High* Good Condition	Average* Fair Condition	Low* Poor Condition	Total
Sleepwear				
Nightgown	_____ $19.00	_____ $12.00	_____ $5.00	_____
Pajamas				
Matching Set	_____ $19.00	_____ $13.00	_____ $5.00	_____
Robe	_____ $30.00	_____ $18.00	_____ $6.00	_____
Teddies	_____ $10.00	_____ $6.00	_____ $5.00	_____
Suits				
Custom Tailored				
Skirt and Jacket	_____ $149.00	_____ $60.00	_____ $20.00	_____
Slacks and Jacket	_____ $139.00	_____ $57.00	_____ $20.00	_____
Jacket	_____ $116.00	_____ $49.00	_____ $24.00	_____
Skirt	_____ $65.00	_____ $40.00	_____ $12.00	_____
Skirt and Jacket	_____ $160.00	_____ $75.00	_____ $36.00	_____
Slacks	_____ $65.00	_____ $24.00	_____ $14.00	_____
Slacks and Jacket	_____ $149.00	_____ $78.00	_____ $38.00	_____
Summerwear				
Shorts				
Denim	_____ $14.00	_____ $8.00	_____ $6.00	_____
Other	_____ $12.00	_____ $8.00	_____ $6.00	_____
Swimsuits				
One-Piece	_____ $30.00	_____ $19.00	_____ $6.00	_____
Two Piece	_____ $32.00	_____ $19.00	_____ $6.00	_____
Tops				
Tank	_____ $14.00	_____ $8.00	_____ $4.00	_____
T-Shirt	_____ $19.00	_____ $11.00	_____ $4.00	_____
Other	_____ $14.00	_____ $9.00	_____ $4.00	_____
Sweaters				
Casual				
Cardigan	_____ $39.00	_____ $21.00	_____ $14.00	_____
Pullover	_____ $30.00	_____ $14.00	_____ $6.00	_____
Turtleneck	_____ $20.00	_____ $11.00	_____ $8.00	_____
Vest	_____ $16.00	_____ $9.00	_____ $6.00	_____
V-Neck	_____ $25.00	_____ $19.00	_____ $10.00	_____

See pages 11 & 12 for important information about properly valuing your donated items.

Women's Designer Clothing

Description	High* Good Condition	Average* Fair Condition	Low* Poor Condition	Total
Dress				
Cardigan	_____ $39.00	_____ $21.00	_____ $14.00	_____
Pullover	_____ $30.00	_____ $14.00	_____ $6.00	_____
Turtleneck	_____ $20.00	_____ $11.00	_____ $8.00	_____
Vest	_____ $16.00	_____ $9.00	_____ $6.00	_____
V-Neck	_____ $25.00	_____ $19.00	_____ $10.00	_____
Undergarments				
Slips				
Camisole	_____ $12.00	_____ $5.00	_____ $4.00	_____
Full	_____ $16.00	_____ $8.00	_____ $4.00	_____
Half	_____ $8.00	_____ $6.00	_____ $4.00	_____
TOTAL WOMEN'S DESIGNER CLOTHING			**$**	

See pages 11 & 12 for important information about properly valuing your donated items.

Men's Designer Clothing

Description	High* Good Condition	Average* Fair Condition	Low* Poor Condition	Total
Accessories				
Belts				
Casual	_____ $24.00	_____ $10.00	_____ $2.00	_____
Leather	_____ $19.00	_____ $5.00	_____ $2.00	_____
Hats				
Cowboy	_____ $79.00	_____ $25.00	_____ $8.00	_____
Dress	_____ $29.00	_____ $25.00	_____ $5.00	_____
Ties				
Clip-on	_____ $28.00	_____ $3.00	_____ $1.00	_____
Silk	_____ $17.00	_____ $8.00	_____ $3.00	_____
Other	_____ $15.00	_____ $7.00	_____ $3.00	_____
Exercise				
Jackets				
Fleece	_____ $19.00	_____ $12.00	_____ $6.00	_____
Nylon	_____ $17.00	_____ $6.00	_____ $4.00	_____
Pants				
Fleece	_____ $16.00	_____ $6.00	_____ $4.00	_____
Nylon	_____ $10.00	_____ $6.00	_____ $4.00	_____
Shirts				
Nylon, Long-Sleeve	_____ $38.00	_____ $6.00	_____ $4.00	_____
Sweatshirt, Long-Sleeve	_____ $29.00	_____ $6.00	_____ $4.00	_____
Shorts				
Fleece	_____ $18.00	_____ $6.00	_____ $4.00	_____
Nylon	_____ $9.00	_____ $6.00	_____ $4.00	_____
Suits (Matching Pants and Top)				
Fleece	_____ $35.00	_____ $10.00	_____ $4.00	_____
Nylon	_____ $35.00	_____ $10.00	_____ $4.00	_____
Outerwear				
Casual Jackets				
Cloth	_____ $35.00	_____ $10.00	_____ $6.00	_____
Nylon	_____ $25.00	_____ $10.00	_____ $6.00	_____

See pages 11 & 12 for important information about properly valuing your donated items.

Men's Designer Clothing

Description	High* Good Condition	Average* Fair Condition	Low* Poor Condition	Total
Casual Winter Coats				
Ski	_____ $68.00	_____ $40.00	_____ $10.00	_____
Other	_____ $70.00	_____ $35.00	_____ $10.00	_____
Dress Jackets	_____ $170.00	_____ $130.00	_____ $10.00	_____
Dress Winter Coats				
All Weather	_____ $75.00	_____ $60.00	_____ $15.00	_____
Wool	_____ $150.00	_____ $100.00	_____ $15.00	_____
Other	_____ $90.00	_____ $75.00	_____ $15.00	_____
Leather Coats				
Casual	_____ $220.00	_____ $180.00	_____ $18.00	_____
Dress	_____ $220.00	_____ $180.00	_____ $18.00	_____
Rainwear	_____ $48.00	_____ $10.00	_____ $6.00	_____
Vests				
Down	_____ $22.00	_____ $15.00	_____ $8.00	_____
Swede	_____ $24.00	_____ $16.00	_____ $10.00	_____
Shirts				
Casual				
Long-Sleeve	_____ $19.00	_____ $13.00	_____ $6.00	_____
Short-Sleeve	_____ $16.00	_____ $10.00	_____ $6.00	_____
Turtleneck	_____ $19.00	_____ $8.00	_____ $6.00	_____
Dress				
Long-Sleeve	_____ $24.00	_____ $19.00	_____ $10.00	_____
Short-Sleeve	_____ $19.00	_____ $16.00	_____ $9.00	_____
Sport				
Pullover, Long-Sleeve	_____ $19.00	_____ $6.00	_____ $3.00	_____
Pullover, Short-Sleeve	_____ $19.00	_____ $6.00	_____ $3.00	_____
Shoes and Boots				
Casual				
Shoes, Slip-on	_____ $49.00	_____ $10.00	_____ $5.00	_____
Shoes, wLaces	_____ $49.00	_____ $10.00	_____ $5.00	_____
Dress				
Boots, Leather	_____ $49.00	_____ $9.00	_____ $8.00	_____
Shoes, Slip-on	_____ $33.00	_____ $10.00	_____ $5.00	_____
Shoes, wLaces	_____ $33.00	_____ $10.00	_____ $5.00	_____

See pages 11 & 12 for important information about properly valuing your donated items.

Men's Designer Clothing

Description	High* Good Condition	Average* Fair Condition	Low* Poor Condition	Total
Sport				
Baseball	_____ $14.00	_____ $4.00	_____ $3.00	_____
Boots, Hiking	_____ $50.00	_____ $15.00	_____ $4.00	_____
Boots, Hunting	_____ $48.00	_____ $10.00	_____ $4.00	_____
Boots, Snow	_____ $30.00	_____ $6.00	_____ $3.00	_____
Football or Softball	_____ $16.00	_____ $7.00	_____ $3.00	_____
Golf	_____ $42.00	_____ $10.00	_____ $2.00	_____
Sneakers, Leather	_____ $39.00	_____ $10.00	_____ $3.00	_____
Sneakers, Other	_____ $35.00	_____ $19.00	_____ $3.00	_____
Slacks and Pants				
Casual				
Corduroy	_____ $23.00	_____ $6.00	_____ $3.00	_____
Denim	_____ $30.00	_____ $10.00	_____ $6.00	_____
Other	_____ $20.00	_____ $6.00	_____ $4.00	_____
Dress	_____ $35.00	_____ $6.00	_____ $4.00	_____
Sleepwear				
Pajamas				
Matching Set	_____ $23.00	_____ $9.00	_____ $4.00	_____
Robe	_____ $30.00	_____ $8.00	_____ $6.00	_____
Suits				
Casual				
Sport Coat	_____ $240.00	_____ $180.00	_____ $30.00	_____
Custom Tailored				
Two Piece	_____ $390.00	_____ $270.00	_____ $40.00	_____
Dress				
Coat	_____ $250.00	_____ $160.00	_____ $48.00	_____
Slacks	_____ $40.00	_____ $20.00	_____ $10.00	_____
Two Piece	_____ $390.00	_____ $190.00	_____ $65.00	_____
Vest	_____ $28.00	_____ $20.00	_____ $18.00	_____
Summerwear				
Shirts				
T-Shirt	_____ $10.00	_____ $4.00	_____ $3.00	_____

See pages 11 & 12 for important information about properly valuing your donated items.

Men's Designer Clothing

Description	High* Good Condition	Average* Fair Condition	Low* Poor Condition	Total
Shorts				
Denim	_____ $24.00	_____ $7.00	_____ $3.00	_____
Other	_____ $32.00	_____ $7.00	_____ $4.00	_____
Sweaters				
Casual				
Cardigan	_____ $35.00	_____ $6.00	_____ $4.00	_____
Pullover, Long-Sleeve	_____ $55.00	_____ $13.00	_____ $4.00	_____
Turtleneck	_____ $28.00	_____ $14.00	_____ $4.00	_____
Vest	_____ $36.00	_____ $8.00	_____ $4.00	_____
V-Neck	_____ $35.00	_____ $9.00	_____ $4.00	_____
Dress				
Cardigan	_____ $35.00	_____ $6.00	_____ $4.00	_____
Pullover, Long-Sleeve	_____ $55.00	_____ $13.00	_____ $4.00	_____
Turtleneck	_____ $28.00	_____ $14.00	_____ $4.00	_____
Vest	_____ $36.00	_____ $8.00	_____ $4.00	_____
V-Neck	_____ $35.00	_____ $9.00	_____ $4.00	_____
TOTAL MEN'S DESIGNER CLOTHING			$	

See pages 11 & 12 for important information about properly valuing your donated items.

Jewelry

Description	High* Good Condition	Average* Fair Condition	Low* Poor Condition	Total
Watches				
Chronograph	_____ $28.00	_____ $22.00	_____ $5.00	_____
Data Link	_____ $46.00	_____ $37.00	_____ $7.00	_____
Digital	_____ $26.00	_____ $23.00	_____ $4.00	_____
HUMVEE Extreme Sports	_____ $22.00	_____ $14.00	_____ $4.00	_____
Ironman Sports	_____ $25.00	_____ $19.00	_____ $4.00	_____
Ladies Bracelet	_____ $17.00	_____ $12.00	_____ $3.00	_____
Marathon	_____ $14.00	_____ $11.00	_____ $3.00	_____
Stainless Steel	_____ $26.00	_____ $22.00	_____ $4.00	_____
Youth	_____ $15.00	_____ $13.00	_____ $3.00	_____
Women's Jewelry				
Bracelet				
Glass	_____ $13.00	_____ $10.00	_____ $2.00	_____
Gold	_____ $14.00	_____ $9.00	_____ $2.00	_____
Pearls	_____ $12.00	_____ $9.00	_____ $2.00	_____
Rhinestone	_____ $18.00	_____ $12.00	_____ $3.00	_____
Silver	_____ $11.00	_____ $9.00	_____ $2.00	_____
Brooch				
Gold	_____ $12.00	_____ $9.00	_____ $2.00	_____
Rhinestone	_____ $13.00	_____ $9.00	_____ $2.00	_____
Choker				
Gold	_____ $13.00	_____ $9.00	_____ $2.00	_____
Pearls	_____ $17.00	_____ $11.00	_____ $3.00	_____
Rhinestone	_____ $18.00	_____ $14.00	_____ $3.00	_____
Demi-Parure				
Rhinestone	_____ $29.00	_____ $18.00	_____ $5.00	_____
Earrings				
Floral	_____ $14.00	_____ $9.00	_____ $2.00	_____
Fruit	_____ $24.00	_____ $16.00	_____ $4.00	_____
Glass	_____ $16.00	_____ $11.00	_____ $3.00	_____
Gold	_____ $10.00	_____ $8.00	_____ $2.00	_____
Jelly Belly	_____ $24.00	_____ $13.00	_____ $4.00	_____
Pearls	_____ $11.00	_____ $9.00	_____ $2.00	_____
Rhinestone	_____ $13.00	_____ $9.00	_____ $2.00	_____
Silver	_____ $14.00	_____ $10.00	_____ $2.00	_____

*See pages 11 & 12 for important information about properly valuing your donated items.

Jewelry

Description	High* Good Condition	Average* Fair Condition	Low* Poor Condition	Total
Furclip				
Floral	_____ $51.00	_____ $39.00	_____ $8.00	_____
Rhinestone	_____ $28.00	_____ $12.00	_____ $4.00	_____
Necklace				
Basic	_____ $24.00	_____ $8.00	_____ $4.00	_____
Designer	_____ $50.00	_____ $20.00	_____ $5.00	_____
Parure				
Rhinestone	_____ $45.00	_____ $31.00	_____ $1.00	_____
Ring				
Designer	_____ $30.00	_____ $20.00	_____ $7.00	_____
Set				
Floral	_____ $51.00	_____ $34.00	_____ $8.00	_____
Glass	_____ $29.00	_____ $22.00	_____ $5.00	_____
Pearls	_____ $44.00	_____ $28.00	_____ $7.00	_____
Rhinestone	_____ $35.00	_____ $24.00	_____ $5.00	_____
Silver	_____ $24.00	_____ $18.00	_____ $4.00	_____
Sunglasses	_____ $20.00	_____ $6.00	_____ $3.00	_____
TOTAL JEWELRY			$	

See pages 11 & 12 for important information about properly valuing your donated items.

Baby Supplies

Description	High* Good Condition	Average* Fair Condition	Low* Poor Condition	Total
Baby Monitor				
Evenflo	_____ $11.00	_____ $8.00	_____ $2.00	_____
Fischer Price				
Cordless Nursery Monitor 71562	_____ $13.00	_____ $8.00	_____ $2.00	_____
Direct Link Privacy Monitor 71566	_____ $16.00	_____ $11.00	_____ $3.00	_____
Sound n Lights Monitor	_____ $10.00	_____ $8.00	_____ $2.00	_____
Other	_____ $9.00	_____ $7.00	_____ $2.00	_____
Gerry	_____ $9.00	_____ $7.00	_____ $2.00	_____
Graco	_____ $16.00	_____ $10.00	_____ $3.00	_____
Safety 1st				
Crystal Clear	_____ $10.00	_____ $8.00	_____ $2.00	_____
Video Monitor	_____ $88.00	_____ $63.00	_____ $14.00	_____
Other	_____ $13.00	_____ $9.00	_____ $2.00	_____
Sony	_____ $13.00	_____ $9.00	_____ $2.00	_____
The First Years	_____ $15.00	_____ $10.00	_____ $3.00	_____
Other	_____ $15.00	_____ $10.00	_____ $3.00	_____
Car Seats				
Britax				
Cruiser	_____ $68.00	_____ $38.00	_____ $11.00	_____
Freeway	_____ $99.00	_____ $76.00	_____ $15.00	_____
Roundabout	_____ $170.00	_____ $165.00	_____ $26.00	_____
Century				
1000 STE	_____ $34.00	_____ $29.00	_____ $5.00	_____
Accel 5-Point	_____ $22.00	_____ $18.00	_____ $4.00	_____
Breverra Auto Booster 5 point	_____ $32.00	_____ $25.00	_____ $5.00	_____
Breverra Premiere	_____ $44.00	_____ $37.00	_____ $7.00	_____
Breverra SE booster car seat	_____ $24.00	_____ $20.00	_____ $4.00	_____
Encore	_____ $43.00	_____ $34.00	_____ $7.00	_____
New Century	_____ $39.00	_____ $34.00	_____ $6.00	_____
NextStep	_____ $25.00	_____ $20.00	_____ $4.00	_____
SE 5-point	_____ $23.00	_____ $19.00	_____ $4.00	_____

See pages 11 & 12 for important information about properly valuing your donated items.

Baby Supplies

Description	High* Good Condition	Average* Fair Condition	Low* Poor Condition	Total
Smart-Fit plus	_____ $35.00	_____ $26.00	_____ $6.00	_____
Smart-Fit plus 22	_____ $36.00	_____ $28.00	_____ $6.00	_____
Cosco				
Alpha Omega	_____ $94.00	_____ $90.00	_____ $14.00	_____
Baby Convertible Car Seat	_____ $94.00	_____ $85.00	_____ $14.00	_____
Children's Car Seat Booster	_____ $20.00	_____ $17.00	_____ $3.00	_____
Cosco	_____ $35.00	_____ $31.00	_____ $6.00	_____
High Back booster	_____ $47.00	_____ $35.00	_____ $7.00	_____
Noah's Ark Infant Car Seat	_____ $36.00	_____ $28.00	_____ $6.00	_____
Regal Ride	_____ $43.00	_____ $38.00	_____ $7.00	_____
Touriva	_____ $35.00	_____ $31.00	_____ $6.00	_____
Turnabout	_____ $34.00	_____ $27.00	_____ $5.00	_____
Voyager	_____ $30.00	_____ $21.00	_____ $5.00	_____
Evenflo				
Booster	_____ $18.00	_____ $15.00	_____ $3.00	_____
On My Way	_____ $26.00	_____ $18.00	_____ $4.00	_____
Right Fit	_____ $19.00	_____ $16.00	_____ $3.00	_____
Safe Embrace	_____ $93.00	_____ $81.00	_____ $14.00	_____
Safe Embrace II	_____ $187.00	_____ $138.00	_____ $28.00	_____
Fisher Price				
Double Guard	_____ $25.00	_____ $19.00	_____ $4.00	_____
Grow With Me	_____ $170.00	_____ $120.00	_____ $26.00	_____
Safe Embrace	_____ $92.00	_____ $83.00	_____ $14.00	_____
Gerry				
Snug Ride	_____ $29.00	_____ $21.00	_____ $5.00	_____
Snug Ride DX5	_____ $34.00	_____ $29.00	_____ $5.00	_____
Other	_____ $39.00	_____ $22.00	_____ $4.00	_____
Miscellaneous				
Bassinets	_____ $20.00	_____ $14.00	_____ $3.00	_____
Bibs	_____ $3.00	_____ $1.00	_____ $0.50	_____
Booster Seat	_____ $12.00	_____ $5.00	_____ $2.00	_____
Bottle Dryers	_____ $1.50	_____ $1.00	_____ $0.50	_____

See pages 11 & 12 for important information about properly valuing your donated items.

Baby Supplies

Description	High* Good Condition	Average* Fair Condition	Low* Poor Condition	Total
Bottle Sets	_____ $2.00	_____ $1.50	_____ $1.00	_____
Bottle Warmer	_____ $6.00	_____ $4.00	_____ $2.00	_____
Bumper Pads	_____ $18.00	_____ $6.00	_____ $3.00	_____
Carrier	_____ $25.00	_____ $10.00	_____ $3.00	_____
Changing Pad	_____ $4.00	_____ $2.00	_____ $1.00	_____
Changing Table	_____ $51.00	_____ $25.00	_____ $5.00	_____
Crib	_____ $100.00	_____ $48.00	_____ $18.00	_____
Diaper Bag	_____ $8.00	_____ $5.00	_____ $1.00	_____
Dolls	_____ $18.00	_____ $5.00	_____ $1.00	_____
High Chair	_____ $30.00	_____ $18.00	_____ $5.00	_____
Johnny Jump-Up	_____ $15.00	_____ $8.00	_____ $2.00	_____
Play Mats	_____ $8.00	_____ $6.00	_____ $4.00	_____
Playpen	_____ $35.00	_____ $20.00	_____ $5.00	_____
Potty Chair	_____ $8.00	_____ $5.00	_____ $1.00	_____
Saucer	_____ $12.00	_____ $6.00	_____ $2.00	_____
Scooter	_____ $12.00	_____ $8.00	_____ $3.00	_____
Sling	_____ $15.00	_____ $8.00	_____ $2.00	_____
Swing	_____ $40.00	_____ $20.00	_____ $7.00	_____
Tub	_____ $8.00	_____ $4.00	_____ $1.00	_____
Walker	_____ $20.00	_____ $11.00	_____ $4.00	_____

Safety Gates

Evenflo

Home Decor Walk Through Gate	_____ $65.00	_____ $51.00	_____ $10.00	_____
Soft N Wide Gate	_____ $30.00	_____ $23.00	_____ $5.00	_____

Fisher Price

Step-Lock Gate Model 9151	_____ $43.00	_____ $35.00	_____ $7.00	_____

Safety 1st

Squeeze n Go Baby Gate	_____ $23.00	_____ $16.00	_____ $4.00	_____
Other	_____ $8.00	_____ $6.00	_____ $4.00	_____

Strollers

Baby Jogger

Jogger II	_____ $184.00	_____ $163.00	_____ $28.00	_____

See pages 11 & 12 for important information about properly valuing your donated items.

Baby Supplies

Description	High* Good Condition	Average* Fair Condition	Low* Poor Condition	Total
Graco				
Concord	_____ $72.00	_____ $41.00	_____ $11.00	_____
Duette Classic Twin	_____ $148.00	_____ $111.00	_____ $23.00	_____
Other	_____ $40.00	_____ $25.00	_____ $4.00	_____
TOTAL BABY SUPPLIES			$	

See pages 11 & 12 for important information about properly valuing your donated items.

Electric Appliances – Small

Description	High* Good Condition	Average* Fair Condition	Low* Poor Condition	Total
Air Purifiers				
Duracraft	_____ $23.00	_____ $21.00	_____ $4.00	_____
Enviracaire	_____ $71.00	_____ $40.00	_____ $11.00	_____
Honeywell				
Corner	_____ $54.00	_____ $45.00	_____ $8.00	_____
QuietCare	_____ $88.00	_____ $76.00	_____ $13.00	_____
True	_____ $53.00	_____ $43.00	_____ $8.00	_____
Kenmore	_____ $38.00	_____ $30.00	_____ $6.00	_____
Vornado	_____ $88.00	_____ $80.00	_____ $14.00	_____
Other	_____ $20.00	_____ $7.00	_____ $3.00	_____
Answering Machine				
All	_____ $20.00	_____ $6.00	_____ $2.00	_____
Blender				
Black and Decker	_____ $37.00	_____ $27.00	_____ $6.00	_____
Braun	_____ $18.00	_____ $13.00	_____ $3.00	_____
Hamilton Beach	_____ $15.00	_____ $12.00	_____ $3.00	_____
KitchenAid	_____ $54.00	_____ $49.00	_____ $8.00	_____
Krups	_____ $44.00	_____ $24.00	_____ $7.00	_____
Maverick	_____ $24.00	_____ $20.00	_____ $4.00	_____
Oster	_____ $26.00	_____ $18.00	_____ $4.00	_____
Sunbeam	_____ $18.00	_____ $14.00	_____ $3.00	_____
Ultrex	_____ $60.00	_____ $37.00	_____ $9.00	_____
Waring	_____ $67.00	_____ $51.00	_____ $10.00	_____
White Westinghouse	_____ $14.00	_____ $12.00	_____ $2.00	_____
Other	_____ $15.00	_____ $6.00	_____ $3.00	_____
Boom Box				
All	_____ $40.00	_____ $10.00	_____ $3.00	_____
Bread Maker				
Breadman	_____ $36.00	_____ $27.00	_____ $6.00	_____
Hitachi	_____ $41.00	_____ $30.00	_____ $7.00	_____
Magic Chef	_____ $29.00	_____ $25.00	_____ $5.00	_____
Oster	_____ $40.00	_____ $32.00	_____ $6.00	_____
Regal	_____ $41.00	_____ $30.00	_____ $6.00	_____

*See pages 11 & 12 for important information about properly valuing your donated items.

Electric Appliances – Small

Description	High* Good Condition	Average* Fair Condition	Low* Poor Condition	Total
Sunbeam	_____ $41.00	_____ $37.00	_____ $6.00	_____
Toastmaster	_____ $36.00	_____ $24.00	_____ $6.00	_____
WelBilt	_____ $36.00	_____ $26.00	_____ $6.00	_____
West Bend	_____ $40.00	_____ $24.00	_____ $6.00	_____
Zojirushi	_____ $84.00	_____ $73.00	_____ $13.00	_____
Other	_____ $32.00	_____ $21.00	_____ $7.00	_____
Burger Maker				
All	_____ $11.00	_____ $4.00	_____ $1.00	_____
Can Opener - Electric				
All	_____ $8.00	_____ $4.00	_____ $2.00	_____
Cappucino Maker				
All	_____ $10.00	_____ $8.00	_____ $5.00	_____
Ceiling Fan				
All	_____ $14.00	_____ $12.00	_____ $10.00	_____
Clock Radio				
All	_____ $15.00	_____ $6.00	_____ $2.00	_____
Coffee Bean Grinder				
All	_____ $10.00	_____ $8.00	_____ $5.00	_____
Coffee Maker - Drip				
All	_____ $16.00	_____ $9.00	_____ $3.00	_____
Coffee Maker - Electric				
Bodum	_____ $15.00	_____ $14.00	_____ $3.00	_____
Braun	_____ $33.00	_____ $26.00	_____ $5.00	_____
Bunn	_____ $77.00	_____ $66.00	_____ $12.00	_____
Cuisinart	_____ $76.00	_____ $64.00	_____ $12.00	_____
DeLonghi	_____ $36.00	_____ $21.00	_____ $6.00	_____
Krups	_____ $38.00	_____ $26.00	_____ $6.00	_____
Mr. Coffee	_____ $11.00	_____ $11.00	_____ $2.00	_____
Other	_____ $9.00	_____ $3.00	_____ $1.00	_____

See pages 11 & 12 for important information about properly valuing your donated items.

Electric Appliances – Small

Description	High* Good Condition	Average* Fair Condition	Low* Poor Condition	Total
Crock Pot				
All	_____ $10.00	_____ $6.00	_____ $2.00	_____
Curling Iron				
All	_____ $18.00	_____ $4.00	_____ $1.00	_____
Deep Fryer				
Bravetti	_____ $67.00	_____ $24.00	_____ $10.00	_____
DeLonghi	_____ $77.00	_____ $64.00	_____ $12.00	_____
Oster	_____ $34.00	_____ $30.00	_____ $5.00	_____
Presto	_____ $16.00	_____ $11.00	_____ $3.00	_____
Sunbeam	_____ $57.00	_____ $45.00	_____ $9.00	_____
T-FAL	_____ $46.00	_____ $36.00	_____ $7.00	_____
Other	_____ $13.00	_____ $9.00	_____ $3.00	_____
Dehumidifier				
Kenmore	_____ $87.00	_____ $73.00	_____ $13.00	_____
Whirlpool	_____ $98.00	_____ $92.00	_____ $15.00	_____
Other	_____ $50.00	_____ $13.00	_____ $4.00	_____
Electric Shaver				
Braun				
150	_____ $24.00	_____ $21.00	_____ $4.00	_____
4501	_____ $22.00	_____ $16.00	_____ $4.00	_____
5414	_____ $36.00	_____ $27.00	_____ $6.00	_____
5416	_____ $36.00	_____ $28.00	_____ $6.00	_____
5520	_____ $38.00	_____ $30.00	_____ $6.00	_____
5550	_____ $39.00	_____ $28.00	_____ $6.00	_____
6520	_____ $61.00	_____ $55.00	_____ $9.00	_____
6525	_____ $54.00	_____ $50.00	_____ $8.00	_____
6550	_____ $69.00	_____ $52.00	_____ $11.00	_____
Norelco				
3405LC	_____ $19.00	_____ $16.00	_____ $3.00	_____
3605X	_____ $25.00	_____ $23.00	_____ $4.00	_____
3805XL	_____ $23.00	_____ $17.00	_____ $4.00	_____
561X	_____ $32.00	_____ $20.00	_____ $5.00	_____
5655X	_____ $76.00	_____ $70.00	_____ $12.00	_____
5801XL	_____ $46.00	_____ $42.00	_____ $7.00	_____

See pages 11 & 12 for important information about properly valuing your donated items.

Electric Appliances – Small

Description	High* Good Condition	Average* Fair Condition	Low* Poor Condition	Total
5811XL	_____ $49.00	_____ $42.00	_____ $8.00	_____
5821XL	_____ $47.00	_____ $42.00	_____ $7.00	_____
5841XL	_____ $50.00	_____ $43.00	_____ $8.00	_____
5861XL	_____ $73.00	_____ $61.00	_____ $11.00	_____
5862XL	_____ $56.00	_____ $51.00	_____ $9.00	_____
5885XL	_____ $52.00	_____ $45.00	_____ $8.00	_____
6826XL	_____ $69.00	_____ $65.00	_____ $11.00	_____
6846XL	_____ $74.00	_____ $68.00	_____ $11.00	_____
6865XL	_____ $73.00	_____ $70.00	_____ $11.00	_____
6885XL	_____ $100.00	_____ $95.00	_____ $15.00	_____
6887XL	_____ $101.00	_____ $94.00	_____ $16.00	_____
Panasonic				
ES201	_____ $9.00	_____ $7.00	_____ $2.00	_____
ES205W	_____ $13.00	_____ $9.00	_____ $2.00	_____
ES765T	_____ $45.00	_____ $40.00	_____ $7.00	_____
ES8065	_____ $40.00	_____ $25.00	_____ $6.00	_____
ES8068N	_____ $106.00	_____ $100.00	_____ $16.00	_____
Remington				
DA307	_____ $23.00	_____ $13.00	_____ $4.00	_____
R845	_____ $23.00	_____ $17.00	_____ $4.00	_____
TA3070	_____ $24.00	_____ $17.00	_____ $4.00	_____
TA4570	_____ $30.00	_____ $20.00	_____ $5.00	_____
Other	_____ $20.00	_____ $15.00	_____ $5.00	_____
Food Dehydrator				
American Harvest	_____ $34.00	_____ $27.00	_____ $5.00	_____
Magic Chef	_____ $28.00	_____ $23.00	_____ $4.00	_____
Ronco	_____ $32.00	_____ $26.00	_____ $5.00	_____
Other	_____ $25.00	_____ $14.00	_____ $4.00	_____
Food Processor				
Black and Decker	_____ $23.00	_____ $15.00	_____ $4.00	_____
GE	_____ $19.00	_____ $13.00	_____ $3.00	_____
Hamilton Beach	_____ $24.00	_____ $17.00	_____ $4.00	_____
KitchenAid	_____ $59.00	_____ $50.00	_____ $9.00	_____
Regal	_____ $25.00	_____ $16.00	_____ $4.00	_____
Sears	_____ $15.00	_____ $11.00	_____ $3.00	_____

See pages 11 & 12 for important information about properly valuing your donated items.

Electric Appliances – Small

Description	High* Good Condition	Average* Fair Condition	Low* Poor Condition	Total
Sunbeam	___ $21.00	___ $15.00	___ $4.00	___
Other	___ $25.00	___ $7.00	___ $3.00	___
Food Steamers				
Black and Decker	___ $15.00	___ $12.00	___ $3.00	___
Oster	___ $23.00	___ $21.00	___ $4.00	___
Sunbeam	___ $16.00	___ $11.00	___ $3.00	___
Other	___ $15.00	___ $9.00	___ $3.00	___
George Foreman Grills				
Foreman Grill - The Champ	___ $26.00	___ $21.00	___ $4.00	___
Foreman Grill - X-Large	___ $44.00	___ $37.00	___ $7.00	___
Foreman Grill - XX-Large	___ $65.00	___ $58.00	___ $10.00	___
Fusion Grill	___ $35.00	___ $26.00	___ $6.00	___
Hair Blow Dryer				
All	___ $14.00	___ $5.00	___ $2.00	___
Heater - Room				
All	___ $10.00	___ $6.00	___ $3.00	___
Humidifier				
Bemis	___ $28.00	___ $24.00	___ $5.00	___
Bionaire	___ $26.00	___ $19.00	___ $4.00	___
Duracraft	___ $23.00	___ $20.00	___ $4.00	___
Emerson	___ $22.00	___ $19.00	___ $4.00	___
General-Aire	___ $82.00	___ $55.00	___ $13.00	___
Holmes	___ $23.00	___ $19.00	___ $4.00	___
Honeywell	___ $24.00	___ $21.00	___ $4.00	___
Hunter	___ $61.00	___ $51.00	___ $9.00	___
Kaz	___ $30.00	___ $17.00	___ $5.00	___
Kenmore	___ $37.00	___ $25.00	___ $6.00	___
Lasko	___ $44.00	___ $27.00	___ $7.00	___
Sharper Image	___ $36.00	___ $32.00	___ $6.00	___
Sunbeam	___ $25.00	___ $20.00	___ $4.00	___
Trion	___ $40.00	___ $34.00	___ $6.00	___

See pages 11 & 12 for important information about properly valuing your donated items.

Electric Appliances – Small

Description	High* Good Condition	Average* Fair Condition	Low* Poor Condition	Total
Vornado	_____ $53.00	_____ $38.00	_____ $8.00	_____
Other	_____ $50.00	_____ $35.00	_____ $12.00	_____
Iron				
Black and Decker				
ProFinish	_____ $19.00	_____ $4.00	_____ $3.00	_____
Other	_____ $9.00	_____ $7.00	_____ $2.00	_____
Proctor	_____ $7.00	_____ $4.00	_____ $1.00	_____
Rowenta				
Powerglide	_____ $38.00	_____ $34.00	_____ $6.00	_____
Powerglide 2	_____ $36.00	_____ $31.00	_____ $6.00	_____
Professional	_____ $68.00	_____ $54.00	_____ $11.00	_____
Sunbeam	_____ $11.00	_____ $9.00	_____ $2.00	_____
Other	_____ $9.00	_____ $5.00	_____ $1.00	_____
Juicer				
Acme	_____ $43.00	_____ $26.00	_____ $7.00	_____
Braun	_____ $15.00	_____ $11.00	_____ $3.00	_____
Champion	_____ $65.00	_____ $49.00	_____ $10.00	_____
Cuisinart	_____ $29.00	_____ $19.00	_____ $5.00	_____
Hamilton Beach	_____ $16.00	_____ $12.00	_____ $3.00	_____
Juice Master	_____ $20.00	_____ $13.00	_____ $3.00	_____
JuiceMan	_____ $46.00	_____ $28.00	_____ $7.00	_____
JuiceMan Jr	_____ $37.00	_____ $32.00	_____ $6.00	_____
JuiceMan Pro Series	_____ $51.00	_____ $40.00	_____ $8.00	_____
Kitchen Aid	_____ $23.00	_____ $20.00	_____ $4.00	_____
Kitchen Classics	_____ $75.00	_____ $59.00	_____ $12.00	_____
Krups	_____ $23.00	_____ $15.00	_____ $4.00	_____
Salton	_____ $23.00	_____ $15.00	_____ $4.00	_____
Sanyo	_____ $25.00	_____ $12.00	_____ $4.00	_____
The Genie	_____ $25.00	_____ $18.00	_____ $4.00	_____
Vita Mix 3600 Plus	_____ $46.00	_____ $32.00	_____ $7.00	_____
Welbilt	_____ $38.00	_____ $26.00	_____ $6.00	_____
Other	_____ $25.00	_____ $17.00	_____ $5.00	_____
Kitchen Clock				
All	_____ $9.00	_____ $4.00	_____ $1.00	_____

See pages 11 & 12 for important information about properly valuing your donated items.

Electric Appliances – Small

Description	High* Good Condition	Average* Fair Condition	Low* Poor Condition	Total
Knife - Electric				
All	_____ $9.00	_____ $5.00	_____ $2.00	_____
Mixer - Hand Electric				
All	_____ $10.00	_____ $5.00	_____ $2.00	_____
Mixers				
Black and Decker	_____ $21.00	_____ $13.00	_____ $4.00	_____
Braun	_____ $16.00	_____ $10.00	_____ $3.00	_____
Farberware	_____ $46.00	_____ $24.00	_____ $7.00	_____
Hamilton Beach	_____ $22.00	_____ $14.00	_____ $4.00	_____
KitchenAid	_____ $20.00	_____ $16.00	_____ $3.00	_____
Krups	_____ $20.00	_____ $14.00	_____ $3.00	_____
Oster	_____ $13.00	_____ $10.00	_____ $2.00	_____
Proctor Silex	_____ $10.00	_____ $9.00	_____ $2.00	_____
Sunbeam	_____ $18.00	_____ $13.00	_____ $3.00	_____
Toastmaster	_____ $10.00	_____ $9.00	_____ $2.00	_____
Other	_____ $13.00	_____ $9.00	_____ $2.00	_____
Pasta Maker				
All	_____ $10.00	_____ $5.00	_____ $2.00	_____
Popcorn Popper - Hot Air				
All	_____ $25.00	_____ $6.00	_____ $2.00	_____
Record Player				
All	_____ $25.00	_____ $10.00	_____ $2.00	_____
Rug Shampooer				
All	_____ $39.00	_____ $17.00	_____ $3.00	_____
Sandwich Maker				
Salton	_____ $9.00	_____ $7.00	_____ $2.00	_____
Toastmaster	_____ $11.00	_____ $10.00	_____ $2.00	_____
Skillet - Electric				
All	_____ $16.00	_____ $8.00	_____ $2.00	_____
Slow Cooker				
Hamilton Beach	_____ $23.00	_____ $16.00	_____ $4.00	_____

See pages 11 & 12 for important information about properly valuing your donated items.

Electric Appliances – Small

Description	High* Good Condition	Average* Fair Condition	Low* Poor Condition	Total
Rival	_____ $10.00	_____ $8.00	_____ $2.00	_____
Westbend	_____ $22.00	_____ $14.00	_____ $4.00	_____
Other	_____ $13.00	_____ $7.00	_____ $2.00	_____
Smoke Detector				
Firex	_____ $36.00	_____ $22.00	_____ $6.00	_____
First Alert	_____ $16.00	_____ $13.00	_____ $3.00	_____
Kidde	_____ $19.00	_____ $14.00	_____ $3.00	_____
Simplex	_____ $42.00	_____ $18.00	_____ $7.00	_____
Other	_____ $12.00	_____ $7.00	_____ $2.00	_____
Tape Recorder				
All	_____ $16.00	_____ $8.00	_____ $2.00	_____
Telephones				
All	_____ $16.00	_____ $5.00	_____ $2.00	_____
Toaster				
Black and Decker	_____ $14.00	_____ $11.00	_____ $2.00	_____
Cuisinart	_____ $33.00	_____ $20.00	_____ $5.00	_____
Fiesta	_____ $24.00	_____ $19.00	_____ $4.00	_____
Hamilton Beach	_____ $13.00	_____ $9.00	_____ $2.00	_____
KitchenAid	_____ $50.00	_____ $40.00	_____ $8.00	_____
Krups	_____ $27.00	_____ $23.00	_____ $4.00	_____
Proctor Silex	_____ $9.00	_____ $7.00	_____ $2.00	_____
Rival	_____ $11.00	_____ $9.00	_____ $2.00	_____
Sunbeam	_____ $22.00	_____ $15.00	_____ $4.00	_____
T-FAL	_____ $33.00	_____ $21.00	_____ $5.00	_____
Toastmaster	_____ $14.00	_____ $9.00	_____ $2.00	_____
Vintage	_____ $12.00	_____ $9.00	_____ $2.00	_____
Other	_____ $16.00	_____ $7.00	_____ $3.00	_____
Toaster Oven				
Black and Decker	_____ $20.00	_____ $15.00	_____ $3.00	_____
DeLonghi	_____ $31.00	_____ $25.00	_____ $5.00	_____
Hamilton Beach	_____ $21.00	_____ $15.00	_____ $3.00	_____
Proctor Silex	_____ $16.00	_____ $13.00	_____ $3.00	_____
Toastmaster	_____ $21.00	_____ $16.00	_____ $3.00	_____
Other	_____ $20.00	_____ $5.00	_____ $2.00	_____

See pages 11 & 12 for important information about properly valuing your donated items.

Electric Appliances – Small

Description	High* Good Condition	Average* Fair Condition	Low* Poor Condition	Total
Vacuum - Canister				
All	_____ $25.00	_____ $12.00	_____ $2.00	_____
Vacuum - Hand Held				
All	_____ $36.00	_____ $10.00	_____ $2.00	_____
Vacuum - Shop-Vac				
All	_____ $40.00	_____ $10.00	_____ $3.00	_____
Vacuum - Upright				
Dirt Devil				
Swivel Glide	_____ $25.00	_____ $21.00	_____ $4.00	_____
Eureka				
1934 The Boss	_____ $18.00	_____ $10.00	_____ $3.00	_____
Whirlwind Bagless	_____ $88.00	_____ $70.00	_____ $14.00	_____
Fantom				
Cyclone XT	_____ $127.00	_____ $77.00	_____ $19.00	_____
Fury	_____ $51.00	_____ $35.00	_____ $8.00	_____
Hoover				
Bagless Upright U5280-900	_____ $84.00	_____ $66.00	_____ $13.00	_____
Windtunnel	_____ $184.00	_____ $125.00	_____ $28.00	_____
Oreck				
XL2000	_____ $208.00	_____ $186.00	_____ $32.00	_____
XL2600 Deluxe	_____ $232.00	_____ $190.00	_____ $35.00	_____
XL9100	_____ $123.00	_____ $98.00	_____ $19.00	_____
Rainbow				
SE	_____ $359.00	_____ $290.00	_____ $54.00	_____
SE with PN2	_____ $380.00	_____ $288.00	_____ $57.00	_____
Turbo Tiger	_____ $38.00	_____ $32.00	_____ $6.00	_____
Other	_____ $32.00	_____ $10.00	_____ $3.00	_____
Vaporizer				
All	_____ $39.00	_____ $6.00	_____ $4.00	_____
Waffle Iron				
Salton	_____ $14.00	_____ $12.00	_____ $9.00	_____

See pages 11 & 12 for important information about properly valuing your donated items.

Electric Appliances – Small

Description	High* Good Condition	Average* Fair Condition	Low* Poor Condition	Total
Water Filter				
Brita	_____ $19.00	_____ $13.00	_____ $9.00	_____
Pitcher	_____ $14.00	_____ $10.00	_____ $2.00	_____
Culligan GE	_____ $19.00	_____ $14.00	_____ $3.00	_____
Kenmore	_____ $26.00	_____ $13.00	_____ $4.00	_____
Countertop	_____ $23.00	_____ $17.00	_____ $4.00	_____
Pur	_____ $19.00	_____ $14.00	_____ $3.00	_____
Reverse Osmosis				
4-Stage System	_____ $137.00	_____ $126.00	_____ $21.00	_____
5-Stage System	_____ $134.00	_____ $129.00	_____ $20.00	_____
Osmosis Membrane	_____ $26.00	_____ $20.00	_____ $4.00	_____
Other	_____ $16.00	_____ $13.00	_____ $5.00	_____
TOTAL ELECTRIC APPLIANCES – SMALL			$	

See pages 11 & 12 for important information about properly valuing your donated items.

Electric Appliances – Large

Description	High* Good Condition	Average* Fair Condition	Low* Poor Condition	Total
Air Conditioners				
All	____ $100.00	____ $55.00	____ $25.00	____
Dishwasher				
All	____ $150.00	____ $78.00	____ $10.00	____
Dryer				
All	____ $150.00	____ $90.00	____ $25.00	____
Freezer				
Chest	____ $150.00	____ $100.00	____ $50.00	____
Upright	____ $125.00	____ $40.00	____ $20.00	____
Jenn-Air				
All	____ $95.00	____ $45.00	____ $20.00	____
Microwave Oven				
GE	____ $43.00	____ $31.00	____ $7.00	____
Goldstar	____ $29.00	____ $25.00	____ $5.00	____
Kenmore	____ $37.00	____ $29.00	____ $6.00	____
Samsung	____ $32.00	____ $22.00	____ $5.00	____
Sanyo	____ $36.00	____ $29.00	____ $6.00	____
Sharp	____ $48.00	____ $34.00	____ $7.00	____
Whirlpool	____ $66.00	____ $53.00	____ $10.00	____
Other	____ $45.00	____ $35.00	____ $15.00	____
Oven				
Wall	____ $133.00	____ $58.00	____ $20.00	____
Range				
Double Oven	____ $190.00	____ $100.00	____ $49.00	____
Oven / Microwave	____ $225.00	____ $125.00	____ $20.00	____
Refrigerator				
All	____ $200.00	____ $100.00	____ $40.00	____
Stove				
Electric	____ $150.00	____ $87.00	____ $30.00	____
Gas	____ $150.00	____ $90.00	____ $30.00	____

See pages 11 & 12 for important information about properly valuing your donated items.

Electric Appliances – Large

Description	High* Good Condition	Average* Fair Condition	Low* Poor Condition	Total
Washer / Dryer Set All	____ $280.00	____ $149.00	____ $50.00	_____
Washing Machine All	____ $225.00	____ $100.00	____ $25.00	_____
TOTAL ELECTRIC APPLIANCES – LARGE			**$**	

See pages 11 & 12 for important information about properly valuing your donated items.

Entertainment

Description	High* Good Condition	Average* Fair Condition	Low* Poor Condition	Total
Books				
Audio Books	_____ $13.00	_____ $10.00	_____ $2.00	_____
Cookbook	_____ $8.00	_____ $4.00	_____ $1.00	_____
Encyclopedias				
Set	_____ $30.00	_____ $20.00	_____ $15.00	_____
Print Books				
Hardback	_____ $8.00	_____ $3.00	_____ $1.00	_____
Paperback	_____ $5.00	_____ $2.00	_____ $1.00	_____
Magazines				
Non-Collector Editions	_____ $2.00	_____ $1.00	_____ $1.00	_____
Movies and Videos				
DVD	_____ $16.00	_____ $12.00	_____ $2.00	_____
Exercise	_____ $7.00	_____ $4.00	_____ $2.00	_____
VHS	_____ $8.00	_____ $5.00	_____ $2.00	_____
Music				
Cassettes	_____ $5.00	_____ $2.00	_____ $1.00	_____
CDs	_____ $10.00	_____ $5.00	_____ $1.00	_____
Records				
45s	_____ $2.00	_____ $1.00	_____ $0.50	_____
Albums	_____ $4.00	_____ $2.00	_____ $1.00	_____
TOTAL ENTERTAINMENT			**$**	

See pages 11 & 12 for important information about properly valuing your donated items.

Furniture

Description	High* Good Condition	Average* Fair Condition	Low* Poor Condition	Total
Bed				
Bunk	____ $118.00	____ $75.00	____ $30.00	_____
Rollaway	____ $40.00	____ $15.00	____ $5.00	_____
Bookshelf				
All	____ $80.00	____ $23.00	____ $15.00	_____
Box Springs				
All	____ $24.00	____ $14.00	____ $5.00	_____
Brass Fireplace Tools				
All	____ $20.00	____ $10.00	____ $5.00	_____
Buffet				
All	____ $210.00	____ $99.00	____ $10.00	_____
Chair				
Bean Bag	____ $10.00	____ $6.00	____ $2.00	_____
Folding Lawn	____ $8.00	____ $4.00	____ $3.00	_____
Living Room	____ $100.00	____ $30.00	____ $14.00	_____
Lounge	____ $103.00	____ $40.00	____ $9.00	_____
Office	____ $50.00	____ $20.00	____ $7.00	_____
Recliner	____ $85.00	____ $34.00	____ $14.00	_____
Secretary	____ $29.00	____ $18.00	____ $5.00	_____
Chest of Drawers				
All	____ $110.00	____ $49.00	____ $10.00	_____
Coat Rack				
All	____ $30.00	____ $14.00	____ $5.00	_____
Curio				
All	____ $179.00	____ $79.00	____ $25.00	_____
Desk				
Bedroom	____ $100.00	____ $39.00	____ $7.00	_____
Child's	____ $65.00	____ $20.00	____ $7.00	_____
Office Wood	____ $180.00	____ $99.00	____ $10.00	_____
Wicker	____ $100.00	____ $50.00	____ $20.00	_____

See pages 11 & 12 for important information about properly valuing your donated items.

Furniture

Description	High* Good Condition	Average* Fair Condition	Low* Poor Condition	Total
Dining Room Set				
All	____ $420.00	____ $150.00	____ $20.00	_____
Dresser				
Regular	____ $169.00	____ $80.00	____ $10.00	_____
with Mirror	____ $240.00	____ $100.00	____ $20.00	_____
Entertainment Center				
All	____ $150.00	____ $75.00	____ $30.00	_____
Headboard				
Full	____ $75.00	____ $27.00	____ $5.00	_____
King	____ $180.00	____ $46.00	____ $5.00	_____
Queen	____ $100.00	____ $30.00	____ $5.00	_____
Twin	____ $75.00	____ $25.00	____ $5.00	_____
Hutch				
Solid Wood	____ $400.00	____ $140.00	____ $68.00	_____
Lamp				
Desk	____ $40.00	____ $33.00	____ $5.00	_____
Floor	____ $65.00	____ $21.00	____ $3.00	_____
Shades	____ $11.00	____ $5.00	____ $1.00	_____
Swag	____ $25.00	____ $10.00	____ $2.00	_____
Table	____ $60.00	____ $16.00	____ $5.00	_____
Magazine Rack				
All	____ $33.00	____ $8.00	____ $3.00	_____
Mattress				
Full	____ $70.00	____ $45.00	____ $15.00	_____
King	____ $70.00	____ $60.00	____ $25.00	_____
Queen	____ $64.00	____ $50.00	____ $20.00	_____
Twin	____ $60.00	____ $33.00	____ $10.00	_____
Nightstand				
All	____ $69.00	____ $22.00	____ $8.00	_____
Piano				
All	____ $300.00	____ $100.00	____ $25.00	_____

See pages 11 & 12 for important information about properly valuing your donated items.

Furniture

Description	High* Good Condition	Average* Fair Condition	Low* Poor Condition	Total
Rocker				
Swivel	____ $105.00	____ $35.00	____ $10.00	_____
Wooden	____ $120.00	____ $30.00	____ $5.00	_____
Sectional				
All	____ $316.00	____ $140.00	____ $15.00	_____
Sewing Machine				
All	____ $75.00	____ $30.00	____ $10.00	_____
Sofa				
3-Piece Set	____ $429.00	____ $200.00	____ $50.00	_____
Love Seat	____ $350.00	____ $100.00	____ $30.00	_____
Regular	____ $200.00	____ $100.00	____ $24.00	_____
with Recliner	____ $210.00	____ $110.00	____ $50.00	_____
with Sleeper	____ $220.00	____ $120.00	____ $40.00	_____
Stool				
Set of 4	____ $100.00	____ $40.00	____ $16.00	_____
with Vanity	____ $100.00	____ $49.00	____ $5.00	_____
Table				
Card with Chairs	____ $30.00	____ $15.00	____ $10.00	_____
Coffee	____ $100.00	____ $40.00	____ $7.00	_____
Dining	____ $250.00	____ $75.00	____ $10.00	_____
Dining with 4 Chairs	____ $225.00	____ $75.00	____ $25.00	_____
End	____ $120.00	____ $30.00	____ $3.00	_____
Hall with Mirror	____ $120.00	____ $50.00	____ $5.00	_____
Kitchen	____ $80.00	____ $40.00	____ $10.00	_____
Typewriter				
Electric	____ $30.00	____ $15.00	____ $8.00	_____
Manual	____ $10.00	____ $8.00	____ $5.00	_____
TOTAL FURNITURE			**$**	

See pages 11 & 12 for important information about properly valuing your donated items.

Garden Tools

Description	High* Good Condition	Average* Fair Condition	Low* Poor Condition	Total
Miscellaneous				
Anvil Lopper	_____ $15.00	_____ $10.00	_____ $3.00	_____
Bug Zapper	_____ $20.00	_____ $14.00	_____ $3.00	_____
Electric Hedge Trimmer	_____ $35.00	_____ $32.00	_____ $6.00	_____
Electric Leaf Blowers	_____ $39.00	_____ $33.00	_____ $6.00	_____
Garden Tool Set	_____ $11.00	_____ $9.00	_____ $2.00	_____
Gas Hedge Trimmers	_____ $98.00	_____ $82.00	_____ $15.00	_____
Gas Leaf Blowers	_____ $57.00	_____ $50.00	_____ $9.00	_____
Hoe	_____ $19.00	_____ $14.00	_____ $3.00	_____
Lawn Mowers				
Push Mowers	_____ $162.00	_____ $88.00	_____ $5.00	_____
Riding Mowers	_____ $485.00	_____ $389.00	_____ $85.00	_____
Pest Control	_____ $13.00	_____ $10.00	_____ $2.00	_____
Pressure Washer	_____ $28.00	_____ $15.00	_____ $5.00	_____
Rake	_____ $12.00	_____ $9.00	_____ $2.00	_____
Shears	_____ $12.00	_____ $9.00	_____ $2.00	_____
Shovel	_____ $10.00	_____ $8.00	_____ $2.00	_____
Sprinkler	_____ $22.00	_____ $19.00	_____ $4.00	_____
Tillers	_____ $362.00	_____ $222.00	_____ $55.00	_____
Trimmer	_____ $32.00	_____ $26.00	_____ $5.00	_____
Watering Can	_____ $13.00	_____ $11.00	_____ $2.00	_____
Wheelbarrow	_____ $16.00	_____ $13.00	_____ $3.00	_____
TOTAL GARDEN TOOLS			$	

See pages 11 & 12 for important information about properly valuing your donated items.

Household Miscellaneous

Description	High* Good Condition	Average* Fair Condition	Low* Poor Condition	Total
Bathroom Miscellaneous				
Bathroom Scale	_____ $10.00	_____ $6.00	_____ $1.00	_____
Shower Curtain	_____ $15.00	_____ $4.00	_____ $1.00	_____
Toilet				
Cover	_____ $4.00	_____ $2.00	_____ $1.00	_____
Floor Mat	_____ $5.00	_____ $3.00	_____ $1.00	_____
Tank Cover	_____ $5.00	_____ $3.00	_____ $1.00	_____
Kitchen Miscellaneous				
Coffee Mug	_____ $3.00	_____ $2.00	_____ $1.00	_____
Cutting Board (Wooden)	_____ $5.00	_____ $2.00	_____ $1.00	_____
Designer Plates	_____ $18.00	_____ $10.00	_____ $2.00	_____
Glassware Tumbler	_____ $3.00	_____ $1.00	_____ $0.50	_____
Hot Pad	_____ $4.00	_____ $2.00	_____ $1.00	_____
Pans	_____ $20.00	_____ $9.00	_____ $1.00	_____
Plates	_____ $6.00	_____ $2.00	_____ $1.00	_____
Shakers - Salt/Pepper	_____ $8.00	_____ $2.00	_____ $1.00	_____
Teapot	_____ $10.00	_____ $5.00	_____ $1.00	_____
Tupperware Bowls	_____ $5.00	_____ $2.00	_____ $1.00	_____
Luggage				
Backpack	_____ $15.00	_____ $7.00	_____ $1.00	_____
Carry-On Bag	_____ $20.00	_____ $9.00	_____ $5.00	_____
Old Set	_____ $50.00	_____ $22.00	_____ $3.00	_____
Suitcase	_____ $20.00	_____ $7.00	_____ $2.00	_____
Miscellaneous				
Ash Tray	_____ $5.00	_____ $2.00	_____ $1.00	_____
Bedroom Curtains	_____ $18.00	_____ $6.00	_____ $2.00	_____
Crutches	_____ $9.00	_____ $6.00	_____ $3.00	_____
Dining Room Drapes	_____ $30.00	_____ $18.00	_____ $3.00	_____
Doormat	_____ $5.00	_____ $3.00	_____ $1.00	_____
Eyeglasses	_____ $12.00	_____ $4.00	_____ $1.00	_____
Flower Pot	_____ $6.00	_____ $2.00	_____ $1.00	_____
Flower Vase (Glass)	_____ $12.00	_____ $2.00	_____ $1.00	_____

See pages 11 & 12 for important information about properly valuing your donated items.

Household Miscellaneous

Description	High* Good Condition		Average* Fair Condition		Low* Poor Condition		Total
Glass Candles	____	$9.00	____	$4.00	____	$1.00	____
Heating Pad	____	$5.00	____	$3.00	____	$1.00	____
Ironing Board	____	$10.00	____	$5.00	____	$2.00	____
Mini Blinds	____	$8.00	____	$3.00	____	$1.00	____
Patterns	____	$3.00	____	$2.00	____	$1.00	____
Picture Frame	____	$12.00	____	$5.00	____	$1.00	____
Straw Baskets	____	$10.00	____	$4.00	____	$1.00	____
TOTAL HOUSEHOLD MISCELLANEOUS						**$**	

See pages 11 & 12 for important information about properly valuing your donated items.

Linens

Description	High* Good Condition	Average* Fair Condition	Low* Poor Condition	Total
Afghan All	_____ $30.00	_____ $9.00	_____ $3.00	_____
Aprons All	_____ $7.00	_____ $3.00	_____ $1.00	_____
Bath Towels All	_____ $8.00	_____ $3.00	_____ $1.00	_____
Bedspread All	_____ $39.00	_____ $17.00	_____ $9.00	_____
Blanket Heating Regular	_____ $12.00 _____ $15.00	_____ $10.00 _____ $8.00	_____ $5.00 _____ $1.00	_____ _____
Comforter All	_____ $40.00	_____ $19.00	_____ $14.00	_____
Dish Towel All	_____ $2.00	_____ $1.00	_____ $0.50	_____
Pillow All	_____ $7.00	_____ $4.00	_____ $1.00	_____
Pillow Sham All	_____ $6.00	_____ $3.00	_____ $1.00	_____
Pillowcase (Set) All	_____ $7.00	_____ $2.00	_____ $1.00	_____
Place Mat (Set) All	_____ $10.00	_____ $3.00	_____ $1.00	_____
Quilt All	_____ $50.00	_____ $30.00	_____ $15.00	_____
Sheets (Set) All	_____ $20.00	_____ $7.00	_____ $3.00	_____
Tablecloth All	_____ $14.00	_____ $6.00	_____ $1.00	_____

See pages 11 & 12 for important information about properly valuing your donated items.

Linens

Description	High* Good Condition	Average* Fair Condition	Low* Poor Condition	Total
Throw Pillows All	_____ $10.00	_____ $4.00	_____ $1.00	_____
Throw Rug All	_____ $20.00	_____ $5.00	_____ $1.00	_____
Washcloth All	_____ $2.00	_____ $1.00	_____ $0.50	_____
TOTAL LINENS				$

See pages 11 & 12 for important information about properly valuing your donated items.

Pets

Description	High* Good Condition		Average* Fair Condition		Low* Poor Condition		Total
Aquariums **and Supplies**							
Air Pump	____	$30.00	____	$14.00	____	$5.00	____
Aquarium Sets	____	$69.00	____	$31.00	____	$11.00	____
Bio-Balls	____	$15.00	____	$10.00	____	$3.00	____
Bio-Sponge Filter	____	$9.00	____	$8.00	____	$2.00	____
Cleaning Tools	____	$11.00	____	$8.00	____	$2.00	____
Decoration, any type	____	$9.00	____	$6.00	____	$2.00	____
Decoration, Gravel	____	$8.00	____	$6.00	____	$2.00	____
Filter	____	$35.00	____	$19.00	____	$6.00	____
Filter Cartridge	____	$6.00	____	$4.00	____	$1.00	____
Filter, Bed	____	$41.00	____	$24.00	____	$6.00	____
Filter, Canister	____	$47.00	____	$30.00	____	$7.00	____
Fish Bowl	____	$13.00	____	$9.00	____	$2.00	____
Fish Food	____	$8.00	____	$5.00	____	$2.00	____
Heater, dry	____	$14.00	____	$10.00	____	$2.00	____
Heater, submersible	____	$16.00	____	$10.00	____	$3.00	____
and Hood	____	$51.00	____	$23.00	____	$8.00	____
Powerhead	____	$21.00	____	$15.00	____	$3.00	____
Protein Skimmer	____	$61.00	____	$35.00	____	$9.00	____
Tank, 10 gallon	____	$15.00	____	$9.00	____	$3.00	____
Tank, 15 gallon	____	$41.00	____	$22.00	____	$6.00	____
Tank, 50 gallon	____	$105.00	____	$64.00	____	$16.00	____
Tank, 55 gallon	____	$99.00	____	$63.00	____	$15.00	____
Tank, 60 gallon	____	$88.00	____	$57.00	____	$14.00	____
Tank, 75 gallon	____	$80.00	____	$42.00	____	$12.00	____
Test Kits	____	$12.00	____	$7.00	____	$2.00	____
Thermometer	____	$13.00	____	$8.00	____	$2.00	____
Supplies							
Bird							
Bowls, Feeder, Water Receptacle	____	$9.00	____	$7.00	____	$2.00	____
Cage	____	$48.00	____	$39.00	____	$8.00	____
Grooming	____	$13.00	____	$8.00	____	$2.00	____

See pages 11 & 12 for important information about properly valuing your donated items.

Pets

Description	High* Good Condition	Average* Fair Condition	Low* Poor Condition	Total
Leashes, Collars, and Leads	_____ $12.00	_____ $8.00	_____ $2.00	_____
Perch	_____ $13.00	_____ $9.00	_____ $2.00	_____
Pet Door	_____ $29.00	_____ $24.00	_____ $5.00	_____
Pet House	_____ $10.00	_____ $8.00	_____ $2.00	_____
Play Gym	_____ $38.00	_____ $15.00	_____ $6.00	_____
Toys	_____ $10.00	_____ $8.00	_____ $2.00	_____
Cat				
Bed	_____ $18.00	_____ $12.00	_____ $3.00	_____
Bowls, Feeder, Water Receptacle	_____ $13.00	_____ $10.00	_____ $2.00	_____
Grooming	_____ $11.00	_____ $8.00	_____ $2.00	_____
Leashes, Collars, and Leads	_____ $8.00	_____ $7.00	_____ $2.00	_____
Litter Box	_____ $19.00	_____ $10.00	_____ $3.00	_____
Litter Box, LitterMaid	_____ $41.00	_____ $16.00	_____ $6.00	_____
Perch	_____ $21.00	_____ $16.00	_____ $3.00	_____
Pet Door	_____ $18.00	_____ $14.00	_____ $3.00	_____
Pet House	_____ $16.00	_____ $12.00	_____ $3.00	_____
Toys	_____ $11.00	_____ $8.00	_____ $2.00	_____
Dog				
Bed	_____ $17.00	_____ $14.00	_____ $3.00	_____
Bowls, Feeder, Water Receptacle	_____ $10.00	_____ $8.00	_____ $2.00	_____
Cage	_____ $41.00	_____ $30.00	_____ $7.00	_____
Grooming	_____ $16.00	_____ $14.00	_____ $3.00	_____
Leashes, Collars, and Leads	_____ $15.00	_____ $10.00	_____ $3.00	_____
No Bark Collar	_____ $43.00	_____ $34.00	_____ $7.00	_____
Pet Door, large	_____ $67.00	_____ $42.00	_____ $10.00	_____
Pet Door, medium	_____ $42.00	_____ $22.00	_____ $7.00	_____
Pet Door, small	_____ $13.00	_____ $11.00	_____ $2.00	_____
Pet House	_____ $23.00	_____ $12.00	_____ $4.00	_____
Toys	_____ $11.00	_____ $9.00	_____ $2.00	_____
Rodent				
Bed	_____ $10.00	_____ $7.00	_____ $2.00	_____
Cage	_____ $27.00	_____ $17.00	_____ $4.00	_____

See pages 11 & 12 for important information about properly valuing your donated items.

Pets

Description	High* Good Condition	Average* Fair Condition	Low* Poor Condition	Total
Fun Tunnel	_____ $10.00	_____ $8.00	_____ $2.00	_____
Leashes, Collars, and Leads	_____ $9.00	_____ $7.00	_____ $2.00	_____
Pet House	_____ $13.00	_____ $9.00	_____ $2.00	_____
TOTAL PETS			**$**	

See pages 11 & 12 for important information about properly valuing your donated items.

Tools

Description	High* Good Condition	Average* Fair Condition	Low* Poor Condition	Total
Adjustable Wrench				
All	_____ $22.00	_____ $12.00	_____ $4.00	_____
Belt Sander				
All	_____ $44.00	_____ $37.00	_____ $7.00	_____
Brad Nailer				
All	_____ $39.00	_____ $25.00	_____ $6.00	_____
Chainsaws				
Craftsman	_____ $77.00	_____ $64.00	_____ $12.00	_____
Echo				
CS3000	_____ $132.00	_____ $121.00	_____ $20.00	_____
CS3400	_____ $155.00	_____ $108.00	_____ $24.00	_____
CS3450	_____ $157.00	_____ $144.00	_____ $24.00	_____
CS4400	_____ $231.00	_____ $210.00	_____ $35.00	_____
Homelite				
20	_____ $164.00	_____ $119.00	_____ $25.00	_____
Husqvarna				
55	_____ $253.00	_____ $198.00	_____ $38.00	_____
136	_____ $158.00	_____ $125.00	_____ $24.00	_____
141	_____ $172.00	_____ $135.00	_____ $26.00	_____
340	_____ $228.00	_____ $201.00	_____ $35.00	_____
350	_____ $266.00	_____ $227.00	_____ $40.00	_____
365	_____ $373.00	_____ $265.00	_____ $56.00	_____
371XP	_____ $363.00	_____ $324.00	_____ $55.00	_____
Poulan				
2050	_____ $73.00	_____ $60.00	_____ $11.00	_____
2150	_____ $98.00	_____ $58.00	_____ $15.00	_____
2550	_____ $107.00	_____ $95.00	_____ $16.00	_____
2750	_____ $119.00	_____ $100.00	_____ $18.00	_____
Poulan 16"	_____ $57.00	_____ $41.00	_____ $9.00	_____
Poulan 20"	_____ $152.00	_____ $127.00	_____ $23.00	_____
Wild Thing	_____ $81.00	_____ $59.00	_____ $12.00	_____
Wood Shark	_____ $68.00	_____ $56.00	_____ $11.00	_____
Woodsman	_____ $78.00	_____ $57.00	_____ $12.00	_____

See pages 11 & 12 for important information about properly valuing your donated items.

Tools

Description	High* Good Condition	Average* Fair Condition	Low* Poor Condition	Total
Stihl				
17	____ $131.00	____ $91.00	____ $20.00	_____
21	____ $152.00	____ $113.00	____ $23.00	_____
25	____ $187.00	____ $150.00	____ $28.00	_____
26	____ $207.00	____ $158.00	____ $31.00	_____
28	____ $173.00	____ $129.00	____ $26.00	_____
31	____ $127.00	____ $95.00	____ $19.00	_____
39	____ $352.00	____ $302.00	____ $53.00	_____
44	____ $439.00	____ $346.00	____ $66.00	_____
018C	____ $140.00	____ $89.00	____ $21.00	_____
019T	____ $172.00	____ $146.00	____ $26.00	_____
020T	____ $294.00	____ $240.00	____ $44.00	_____
036 Pro	____ $395.00	____ $344.00	____ $60.00	_____
Other	____ $45.00	____ $24.00	____ $9.00	_____
Cordless Screwdriver				
All	____ $12.00	____ $6.00	____ $2.00	_____
Crown Stapler				
All	____ $43.00	____ $25.00	____ $7.00	_____
Drywall Power Screwdriver				
All	____ $51.00	____ $36.00	____ $8.00	_____
Finishing Sander				
All	____ $14.00	____ $9.00	____ $2.00	_____
Flashlight				
All	____ $3.00	____ $2.00	____ $1.00	_____
Grinder				
All	____ $25.00	____ $18.00	____ $4.00	_____
Impact Wrench				
All	____ $33.00	____ $24.00	____ $5.00	_____
Level				
All	____ $10.00	____ $7.00	____ $2.00	_____

See pages 11 & 12 for important information about properly valuing your donated items.

Tools

Description	High* Good Condition	Average* Fair Condition	Low* Poor Condition	Total
Orbital Sander				
All	_____ $21.00	_____ $14.00	_____ $3.00	_____
Power Drills				
Bosch				
1194VSR	_____ $56.00	_____ $46.00	_____ $9.00	_____
DeWalt				
DW100	_____ $35.00	_____ $28.00	_____ $6.00	_____
DW106	_____ $33.00	_____ $28.00	_____ $5.00	_____
DW106K	_____ $46.00	_____ $41.00	_____ $7.00	_____
DW130	_____ $72.00	_____ $57.00	_____ $11.00	_____
DW131	_____ $87.00	_____ $63.00	_____ $13.00	_____
DW160	_____ $85.00	_____ $75.00	_____ $13.00	_____
DW235G	_____ $56.00	_____ $42.00	_____ $9.00	_____
DW236	_____ $50.00	_____ $42.00	_____ $8.00	_____
DW236K	_____ $78.00	_____ $65.00	_____ $12.00	_____
DW926K-2	_____ $65.00	_____ $55.00	_____ $10.00	_____
DW953K-2	_____ $90.00	_____ $83.00	_____ $14.00	_____
DW954K-2	_____ $120.00	_____ $110.00	_____ $18.00	_____
DW958K-2	_____ $130.00	_____ $118.00	_____ $20.00	_____
DW965	_____ $123.00	_____ $103.00	_____ $19.00	_____
DW972K-2	_____ $109.00	_____ $96.00	_____ $17.00	_____
DW990K-2	_____ $136.00	_____ $119.00	_____ $21.00	_____
DW995K-2	_____ $172.00	_____ $154.00	_____ $26.00	_____
DW997K-2	_____ $186.00	_____ $174.00	_____ $28.00	_____
DW998K-2	_____ $172.00	_____ $157.00	_____ $26.00	_____
MaKita				
6406	_____ $32.00	_____ $27.00	_____ $5.00	_____
6343DWAE	_____ $170.00	_____ $152.00	_____ $26.00	_____
DA3000R	_____ $86.00	_____ $77.00	_____ $13.00	_____
DA391D	_____ $73.00	_____ $52.00	_____ $11.00	_____
DA6300	_____ $137.00	_____ $116.00	_____ $21.00	_____
Milwaukee				
0375-6	_____ $78.00	_____ $73.00	_____ $12.00	_____
0512-21	_____ $111.00	_____ $70.00	_____ $17.00	_____
0522-20	_____ $101.00	_____ $82.00	_____ $15.00	_____

See pages 11 & 12 for important information about properly valuing your donated items.

Tools

Description	High* Good Condition	Average* Fair Condition	Low* Poor Condition	Total
1101-1	_____ $97.00	_____ $78.00	_____ $15.00	_____
1107-1	_____ $146.00	_____ $129.00	_____ $22.00	_____
1675-6	_____ $197.00	_____ $166.00	_____ $30.00	_____
1676-6	_____ $219.00	_____ $202.00	_____ $33.00	_____
1854-1	_____ $119.00	_____ $71.00	_____ $18.00	_____
3107-6	_____ $172.00	_____ $162.00	_____ $26.00	_____
Porter Cable				
7556	_____ $115.00	_____ $97.00	_____ $18.00	_____
Other	_____ $35.00	_____ $25.00	_____ $9.00	_____
Router				
All	_____ $33.00	_____ $26.00	_____ $5.00	_____
Router Bits				
All	_____ $10.00	_____ $7.00	_____ $2.00	_____
TOTAL TOOLS			**$**	

See pages 11 & 12 for important information about properly valuing your donated items.

Exercise Equipment

Description	High* Good Condition	Average* Fair Condition	Low* Poor Condition	Total
Abdominal Equipment				
Ab Flex	____ $8.00	____ $5.00	____ $2.00	____
Ab Max	____ $7.00	____ $4.00	____ $1.00	____
Ab Rocker	____ $3.00	____ $2.00	____ $1.00	____
Ab Roller	____ $13.00	____ $9.00	____ $2.00	____
Ab Roller Plus	____ $28.00	____ $21.00	____ $5.00	____
Ab Slide	____ $12.00	____ $10.00	____ $2.00	____
Ab Wheel	____ $13.00	____ $10.00	____ $2.00	____
Fitness Quest Flexa Ball	____ $22.00	____ $14.00	____ $4.00	____
Fitness Quest Torso Track	____ $106.00	____ $83.00	____ $16.00	____
Fitness Quest Torso Track 2	____ $51.00	____ $47.00	____ $8.00	____
Nordic Track Ab Works	____ $44.00	____ $32.00	____ $7.00	____
Richard Simmons AB Formula	____ $7.00	____ $6.00	____ $1.00	____
Exercise Machines				
Cross Country Ski Machine	____ $99.00	____ $80.00	____ $18.00	____
Exercise Bikes				
Computerized	____ $95.00	____ $29.00	____ $10.00	____
Manual	____ $50.00	____ $20.00	____ $7.00	____
Nordic Track	____ $200.00	____ $48.00	____ $29.00	____
Rowing Machine	____ $50.00	____ $17.00	____ $7.00	____
Stair Masters				
Computerized	____ $84.00	____ $40.00	____ $10.00	____
Manual	____ $50.00	____ $25.00	____ $5.00	____
Treadmill				
Computerized	____ $280.00	____ $55.00	____ $10.00	____
Miscellaneous				
Bar Bells with Weights	____ $68.00	____ $23.00	____ $5.00	____
Exercise Ball	____ $21.00	____ $18.00	____ $4.00	____

See pages 11 & 12 for important information about properly valuing your donated items.

Exercise Equipment

Description	High* Good Condition	Average* Fair Condition	Low* Poor Condition	Total
Hand and Ankle Weights	_____ $7.00	_____ $5.00	_____ $4.00	_____
Heart Rate Monitor	_____ $54.00	_____ $43.00	_____ $12.00	_____
Jump Rope	_____ $9.00	_____ $5.00	_____ $1.00	_____
Weight Belt	_____ $12.00	_____ $9.00	_____ $5.00	_____
Weight Bench	_____ $75.00	_____ $20.00	_____ $10.00	_____
TOTAL EXERCISE EQUIPMENT				**$**

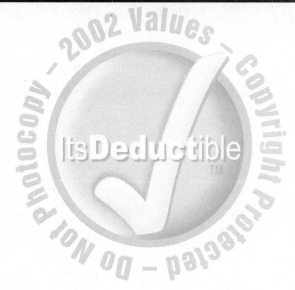

See pages 11 & 12 for important information about properly valuing your donated items.

Sporting Goods

Description	High* Good Condition	Average* Fair Condition	Low* Poor Condition	Total
Baseball / Softball Equipment				
Baseball	____ $1.50	____ $1.00	____ $0.50	_____
Bases	____ $14.00	____ $4.00	____ $1.00	_____
Bat				
Aluminum	____ $23.00	____ $8.00	____ $2.00	_____
Wood	____ $10.00	____ $5.00	____ $2.00	_____
Bat Bag	____ $12.00	____ $5.00	____ $1.00	_____
Batters Helmet	____ $10.00	____ $5.00	____ $1.00	_____
Catchers				
Chest Protector	____ $28.00	____ $10.00	____ $2.00	_____
Mask	____ $24.00	____ $10.00	____ $2.00	_____
Shin Guards	____ $20.00	____ $6.00	____ $2.00	_____
Glove				
Catchers	____ $85.00	____ $8.00	____ $3.00	_____
Fielders	____ $60.00	____ $7.00	____ $3.00	_____
Pants	____ $10.00	____ $5.00	____ $2.00	_____
Pitchback	____ $15.00	____ $10.00	____ $8.00	_____
Shoes	____ $15.00	____ $6.00	____ $3.00	_____
Softball	____ $4.00	____ $1.00	____ $0.50	_____
Stirrup Socks	____ $7.00	____ $3.00	____ $1.00	_____
Umpires Chest Protector	____ $29.00	____ $10.00	____ $3.00	_____
Basketball Equipment				
Basketball	____ $8.00	____ $4.00	____ $1.00	
Biking Equipment				
Bike	____ $80.00	____ $23.00	____ $10.00	_____
Bike Carrier	____ $30.00	____ $10.00	____ $5.00	
Tricycle	____ $15.00	____ $10.00	____ $3.00	
Billiards Equipment				
Cue Stick	____ $8.00	____ $6.00	____ $2.00	_____
Pool Balls (Set)	____ $62.00	____ $22.00	____ $8.00	_____

See pages 11 & 12 for important information about properly valuing your donated items.

Sporting Goods

Description	High* Good Condition	Average* Fair Condition	Low* Poor Condition	Total
Bowling Equipment				
Bag	_____ $14.00	_____ $5.00	_____ $1.00	_____
Ball	_____ $12.00	_____ $6.00	_____ $2.00	_____
Shoes	_____ $10.00	_____ $5.00	_____ $3.00	_____
Boxing Equipment				
Gloves				
Other	_____ $13.00	_____ $5.00	_____ $2.00	_____
Century	_____ $9.00	_____ $8.00	_____ $2.00	_____
Everlast	_____ $12.00	_____ $10.00	_____ $2.00	_____
TKO	_____ $17.00	_____ $11.00	_____ $3.00	_____
Head Gear	_____ $16.00	_____ $11.00	_____ $8.00	_____
Jump Rope	_____ $10.00	_____ $7.00	_____ $5.00	_____
Punching Bag	_____ $46.00	_____ $33.00	_____ $7.00	_____
Speed Bag	_____ $24.00	_____ $17.00	_____ $11.00	_____
Camping Equipment				
Air Mattresses	_____ $21.00	_____ $16.00	_____ $4.00	_____
Coolers				
Coleman	_____ $33.00	_____ $19.00	_____ $5.00	_____
Igloo	_____ $27.00	_____ $11.00	_____ $4.00	_____
Thermos Cooler	_____ $18.00	_____ $9.00	_____ $3.00	_____
Fishing Lures	_____ $4.00	_____ $2.00	_____ $1.00	_____
Fishing Rod and Reel				
Adults	_____ $20.00	_____ $12.00	_____ $4.00	_____
Child's	_____ $8.00	_____ $4.00	_____ $1.00	_____
Heaters	_____ $28.00	_____ $19.00	_____ $5.00	_____
Lanterns				
Coleman	_____ $25.00	_____ $14.00	_____ $4.00	_____
Freeplay	_____ $23.00	_____ $21.00	_____ $4.00	_____
Optimus	_____ $114.00	_____ $56.00	_____ $17.00	_____
Petro Max	_____ $82.00	_____ $43.00	_____ $13.00	_____
Other	_____ $12.00	_____ $7.00	_____ $3.00	_____
Plastic Cooler				
Large	_____ $10.00	_____ $5.00	_____ $3.00	_____

See pages 11 & 12 for important information about properly valuing your donated items.

Sporting Goods

Description	High* Good Condition	Average* Fair Condition	Low* Poor Condition	Total
Sleeping Bags				
L.L. Bean	_____ $29.00	_____ $15.00	_____ $5.00	_____
La Fuma	_____ $87.00	_____ $66.00	_____ $13.00	_____
The North Face	_____ $78.00	_____ $51.00	_____ $12.00	_____
White Stag	_____ $28.00	_____ $16.00	_____ $5.00	_____
Other	_____ $20.00	_____ $8.00	_____ $4.00	_____
Stoves				
Athena International	_____ $214.00	_____ $113.00	_____ $32.00	_____
Camping Gaz	_____ $11.00	_____ $7.00	_____ $2.00	_____
Coleman	_____ $28.00	_____ $17.00	_____ $4.00	_____
Glow Master	_____ $22.00	_____ $17.00	_____ $4.00	_____
Other	_____ $10.00	_____ $6.50	_____ $3.50	_____
Tents				
Coleman	_____ $44.00	_____ $29.00	_____ $7.00	_____
Marmot	_____ $238.00	_____ $192.00	_____ $36.00	_____
Moss	_____ $25.00	_____ $8.00	_____ $4.00	_____
Mountain Hardware	_____ $241.00	_____ $181.00	_____ $37.00	_____
Sierra Designs	_____ $128.00	_____ $81.00	_____ $20.00	_____
The North Face	_____ $197.00	_____ $148.00	_____ $30.00	_____
Other	_____ $25.00	_____ $18.00	_____ $7.00	_____
Football Equipment				
Football	_____ $12.00	_____ $5.00	_____ $1.00	_____
Helmet	_____ $12.00	_____ $5.00	_____ $1.00	_____
Pads	_____ $28.00	_____ $5.00	_____ $3.00	_____
Shoes	_____ $30.00	_____ $10.00	_____ $3.00	_____
Golfing Equipment				
Bag				
Bennington	_____ $54.00	_____ $32.00	_____ $8.00	_____
Burton	_____ $34.00	_____ $24.00	_____ $5.00	_____
Callaway	_____ $49.00	_____ $27.00	_____ $8.00	_____
Datrek	_____ $47.00	_____ $28.00	_____ $7.00	_____
Jones	_____ $35.00	_____ $23.00	_____ $6.00	_____
Karsten Ping	_____ $55.00	_____ $34.00	_____ $9.00	_____
Nicklaus	_____ $46.00	_____ $29.00	_____ $7.00	_____

See pages 11 & 12 for important information about properly valuing your donated items.

Sporting Goods

Description	High* Good Condition	Average* Fair Condition	Low* Poor Condition	Total
Nike	_____ $42.00	_____ $22.00	_____ $7.00	_____
Ogio	_____ $116.00	_____ $81.00	_____ $18.00	_____
Sun Mountain	_____ $65.00	_____ $43.00	_____ $10.00	_____
Taylor Made	_____ $46.00	_____ $29.00	_____ $7.00	_____
Top-Flite	_____ $51.00	_____ $29.00	_____ $8.00	_____
Wilson	_____ $53.00	_____ $32.00	_____ $8.00	_____
Other	_____ $50.00	_____ $15.00	_____ $2.00	_____
Ball	_____ $1.50	_____ $1.00	_____ $0.50	_____
Club Covers	_____ $10.00	_____ $5.00	_____ $1.00	_____
Clubs				
8-Piece Set	_____ $160.00	_____ $30.00	_____ $8.00	_____
Iron	_____ $20.00	_____ $7.00	_____ $2.00	_____
Putter	_____ $33.00	_____ $8.00	_____ $2.00	_____
Wood	_____ $65.00	_____ $8.00	_____ $2.00	_____
Pull Cart	_____ $20.00	_____ $10.00	_____ $3.00	_____
Shoes	_____ $20.00	_____ $10.00	_____ $3.00	_____

Hockey Equipment

Description	High*	Average*	Low*	Total
Gloves	_____ $48.00	_____ $10.00	_____ $2.00	_____
Goal	_____ $29.00	_____ $5.00	_____ $1.00	_____
Goalie Pads	_____ $65.00	_____ $10.00	_____ $3.00	_____
Helmet	_____ $30.00	_____ $9.00	_____ $2.00	_____
Insulated Pants	_____ $40.00	_____ $10.00	_____ $3.00	_____
Shoulder Pads	_____ $34.00	_____ $9.00	_____ $3.00	_____
Stick	_____ $30.00	_____ $5.00	_____ $2.00	_____

Hockey Skates

Description	High*	Average*	Low*	Total
Bauer				
Black Panther	_____ $23.00	_____ $12.00	_____ $4.00	_____
Challenger	_____ $19.00	_____ $10.00	_____ $3.00	_____
Charger	_____ $21.00	_____ $17.00	_____ $4.00	_____
Reactor 5000 Goalie	_____ $116.00	_____ $74.00	_____ $18.00	_____
Supreme 100	_____ $29.00	_____ $23.00	_____ $5.00	_____
Supreme 1000	_____ $49.00	_____ $35.00	_____ $8.00	_____
Supreme 2000	_____ $39.00	_____ $22.00	_____ $6.00	_____

See pages 11 & 12 for important information about properly valuing your donated items.

Sporting Goods

Description	High* Good Condition	Average* Fair Condition	Low* Poor Condition	Total
Supreme 3000	_____ $60.00	_____ $39.00	_____ $9.00	_____
Supreme 4000	_____ $95.00	_____ $50.00	_____ $15.00	_____
Supreme 5000	_____ $117.00	_____ $79.00	_____ $18.00	_____
Supreme 7000	_____ $152.00	_____ $108.00	_____ $23.00	_____
Vapor 10	_____ $228.00	_____ $185.00	_____ $34.00	_____
Vapor 8	_____ $124.00	_____ $100.00	_____ $19.00	_____
CCM				
101	_____ $23.00	_____ $15.00	_____ $4.00	_____
952	_____ $68.00	_____ $43.00	_____ $11.00	_____
1052	_____ $157.00	_____ $133.00	_____ $24.00	_____
652 Black Tacks	_____ $63.00	_____ $51.00	_____ $10.00	_____
Champion 90 Men's	_____ $27.00	_____ $18.00	_____ $4.00	_____
Rapide 101	_____ $26.00	_____ $8.00	_____ $4.00	_____
Ultra 100	_____ $28.00	_____ $18.00	_____ $4.00	_____
Daoust				
National 301	_____ $41.00	_____ $21.00	_____ $6.00	_____
Easton				
Air	_____ $53.00	_____ $32.00	_____ $8.00	_____
Ultra Lite	_____ $58.00	_____ $37.00	_____ $9.00	_____
Ultra Lite Pro	_____ $70.00	_____ $52.00	_____ $11.00	_____
Graf				
703	_____ $127.00	_____ $99.00	_____ $19.00	_____
705	_____ $156.00	_____ $103.00	_____ $24.00	_____
707	_____ $185.00	_____ $153.00	_____ $28.00	_____
Mission				
Amp 4	_____ $84.00	_____ $68.00	_____ $13.00	_____
Amp 5	_____ $65.00	_____ $51.00	_____ $10.00	_____
Amp 6	_____ $79.00	_____ $51.00	_____ $12.00	_____
Amp 7	_____ $57.00	_____ $44.00	_____ $9.00	_____
Flyweight	_____ $168.00	_____ $128.00	_____ $26.00	_____

See pages 11 & 12 for important information about properly valuing your donated items.

Sporting Goods

Description	High* Good Condition	Average* Fair Condition	Low* Poor Condition	Total
Nike				
Ignite 2 Sr.	_____ $67.00	_____ $46.00	_____ $10.00	_____
Ignite 7 Sr.	_____ $76.00	_____ $66.00	_____ $12.00	_____
Zoom Air	_____ $51.00	_____ $38.00	_____ $8.00	_____
Other	_____ $50.00	_____ $10.00	_____ $3.00	_____
Miscellaneous				
Baby Jogger	_____ $129.00	_____ $89.00	_____ $21.00	_____
Badminton Racquet	_____ $5.00	_____ $1.50	_____ $1.00	_____
Frisbees	_____ $3.00	_____ $1.00	_____ $0.50	_____
Trophies	_____ $4.00	_____ $2.00	_____ $1.00	_____
Racquetball Equipment				
Balls	_____ $2.00	_____ $1.00	_____ $0.50	_____
Skates - Inline				
Bauer				
H 3	_____ $34.00	_____ $31.00	_____ $5.00	_____
Vapor 3	_____ $104.00	_____ $74.00	_____ $16.00	_____
Bont				
Labeda Verducci	_____ $137.00	_____ $88.00	_____ $21.00	_____
Sharkie	_____ $93.00	_____ $52.00	_____ $14.00	_____
K2				
125	_____ $103.00	_____ $83.00	_____ $16.00	_____
Ascent	_____ $49.00	_____ $33.00	_____ $8.00	_____
Backyard Bob	_____ $67.00	_____ $49.00	_____ $10.00	_____
Bing Air	_____ $89.00	_____ $79.00	_____ $14.00	_____
Camano	_____ $59.00	_____ $48.00	_____ $9.00	_____
Catalyst	_____ $114.00	_____ $80.00	_____ $17.00	_____
Escape	_____ $75.00	_____ $60.00	_____ $12.00	_____
Exotech	_____ $68.00	_____ $48.00	_____ $11.00	_____
Fatty	_____ $89.00	_____ $51.00	_____ $14.00	_____
Fatty Pro	_____ $79.00	_____ $53.00	_____ $12.00	_____

See pages 11 & 12 for important information about properly valuing your donated items.

Sporting Goods

Description	High* Good Condition	Average* Fair Condition	Low* Poor Condition	Total
Flight 76	_____ $54.00	_____ $40.00	_____ $8.00	_____
Flight ALX	_____ $93.00	_____ $68.00	_____ $14.00	_____
Flight In line Skates	_____ $59.00	_____ $44.00	_____ $9.00	_____
K2 Aggressive Skates	_____ $77.00	_____ $56.00	_____ $12.00	_____
Merlin	_____ $38.00	_____ $27.00	_____ $6.00	_____
Reflex	_____ $49.00	_____ $40.00	_____ $8.00	_____
Velocity	_____ $90.00	_____ $57.00	_____ $14.00	_____
Mission				
Proto V	_____ $52.00	_____ $30.00	_____ $8.00	_____
Nike				
Zoom Air	_____ $51.00	_____ $42.00	_____ $8.00	_____
Roces				
5th Element	_____ $70.00	_____ $53.00	_____ $11.00	_____
Khuti	_____ $135.00	_____ $100.00	_____ $21.00	_____
Tokyo	_____ $34.00	_____ $30.00	_____ $5.00	_____
Rollerblade				
Aggressive Skates	_____ $52.00	_____ $39.00	_____ $8.00	_____
Blade Runner	_____ $25.00	_____ $20.00	_____ $4.00	_____
Burner	_____ $43.00	_____ $33.00	_____ $7.00	_____
Coyote	_____ $70.00	_____ $64.00	_____ $11.00	_____
Derby	_____ $61.00	_____ $60.00	_____ $10.00	_____
Dirk Aggressive	_____ $58.00	_____ $34.00	_____ $9.00	_____
Hydrus Beta	_____ $48.00	_____ $32.00	_____ $8.00	_____
Kitalpha Delta SX	_____ $59.00	_____ $37.00	_____ $9.00	_____
Macroblades	_____ $35.00	_____ $21.00	_____ $6.00	_____
Outback	_____ $58.00	_____ $37.00	_____ $9.00	_____
Rollerblade Lightning TRS	_____ $32.00	_____ $26.00	_____ $5.00	_____
Triax	_____ $45.00	_____ $39.00	_____ $7.00	_____
Viablade Parkway	_____ $37.00	_____ $30.00	_____ $6.00	_____
Salomon				
ST 8 Aggressive Skates	_____ $88.00	_____ $67.00	_____ $14.00	_____
ST 9	_____ $112.00	_____ $81.00	_____ $17.00	_____
ST 90	_____ $110.00	_____ $70.00	_____ $17.00	_____
TR Inline Racing Skates	_____ $189.00	_____ $162.00	_____ $29.00	_____

See pages 11 & 12 for important information about properly valuing your donated items.

Sporting Goods

Description	High* Good Condition	Average* Fair Condition	Low* Poor Condition	Total
Other				
Adult	_____ $40.00	_____ $14.00	_____ $5.00	_____
Child	_____ $28.00	_____ $11.00	_____ $5.00	_____
Skating Equipment				
Ice Skates				
Adult	_____ $25.00	_____ $10.00	_____ $3.00	_____
Child	_____ $30.00	_____ $13.00	_____ $3.00	_____
Roller Racers	_____ $15.00	_____ $7.00	_____ $5.00	_____
Roller Skates	_____ $25.00	_____ $8.00	_____ $3.00	_____
Skate Bag	_____ $6.00	_____ $4.00	_____ $1.00	_____
Skate Board	_____ $30.00	_____ $10.00	_____ $3.00	_____
Skate Knee Pads	_____ $8.00	_____ $4.00	_____ $1.00	_____
Ski Equipment				
Snow Skiing				
Ski Board	_____ $49.00	_____ $12.00	_____ $3.00	_____
Ski Boot Carrier	_____ $35.00	_____ $9.00	_____ $1.00	_____
Ski Boots - Adult	_____ $35.00	_____ $11.00	_____ $4.00	_____
Ski Boots - Child	_____ $20.00	_____ $10.00	_____ $3.00	_____
Ski Glider	_____ $36.00	_____ $10.00	_____ $7.00	_____
Ski Goggles	_____ $19.00	_____ $9.00	_____ $3.00	_____
Ski Poles	_____ $14.00	_____ $5.00	_____ $2.00	_____
Skis (Pair)	_____ $65.00	_____ $13.00	_____ $7.00	_____
Water Skiing				
Knee Board	_____ $30.00	_____ $12.00	_____ $7.00	_____
Water-Ski (Pair)	_____ $50.00	_____ $20.00	_____ $7.00	_____
Water-Ski (Slalom)	_____ $38.00	_____ $12.00	_____ $7.00	_____
Soccer Equipment				
Ball	_____ $7.00	_____ $3.00	_____ $1.00	_____
Shin Guards	_____ $10.00	_____ $4.00	_____ $1.00	_____
Tennis Equipment				
Can of Balls	_____ $3.00	_____ $1.50	_____ $0.50	_____

See pages 11 & 12 for important information about properly valuing your donated items.

Sporting Goods

Description	High* Good Condition	Average* Fair Condition	Low* Poor Condition	Total
Racquet				
Graphite	_____ $28.00	_____ $6.00	_____ $2.00	_____
Wood	_____ $9.00	_____ $3.00	_____ $1.00	_____
TOTAL SPORTING GOODS			$	

*See pages 11 & 12 for important information about properly valuing your donated items.

Games

Description	High* Good Condition	Average* Fair Condition	Low* Poor Condition	Total
Board Games				
Axis and Allies	_____ $24.00	_____ $19.00	_____ $4.00	_____
Bamboozle	_____ $5.00	_____ $3.00	_____ $1.00	_____
Battle of the Sexes	_____ $13.00	_____ $10.00	_____ $2.00	_____
Battleship	_____ $5.00	_____ $3.00	_____ $1.00	_____
Battleship 1967	_____ $5.00	_____ $3.00	_____ $1.00	_____
Battleship 1971	_____ $4.00	_____ $3.00	_____ $1.00	_____
Battleship 1978	_____ $4.00	_____ $3.00	_____ $1.00	_____
Beyond Balderdash	_____ $9.00	_____ $8.00	_____ $2.00	_____
Boggle	_____ $15.00	_____ $8.00	_____ $3.00	_____
Brain Quest	_____ $6.00	_____ $5.00	_____ $1.00	_____
Candyland	_____ $15.00	_____ $7.00	_____ $3.00	_____
Carmen Sandiego USA	_____ $6.00	_____ $4.00	_____ $1.00	_____
Carmen Sandiego World	_____ $6.00	_____ $5.00	_____ $1.00	_____
Castle Risk	_____ $22.00	_____ $15.00	_____ $4.00	_____
Catch Phrase	_____ $18.00	_____ $12.00	_____ $3.00	_____
Challenge Yahtzee	_____ $5.00	_____ $3.00	_____ $1.00	_____
Cheers	_____ $13.00	_____ $5.00	_____ $2.00	_____
Cheers Trivia	_____ $8.00	_____ $5.00	_____ $2.00	_____
Chutes and Ladders	_____ $9.00	_____ $5.00	_____ $2.00	_____
Clue	_____ $21.00	_____ $9.00	_____ $3.00	_____
Clue Junior	_____ $6.00	_____ $4.00	_____ $1.00	_____
Cranium	_____ $25.00	_____ $18.00	_____ $4.00	_____
Don't be a Dork	_____ $19.00	_____ $14.00	_____ $3.00	_____
Don't Wake Daddy	_____ $6.00	_____ $4.00	_____ $1.00	_____
Electronic Battleship	_____ $11.00	_____ $8.00	_____ $2.00	_____
Game of Life	_____ $15.00	_____ $8.00	_____ $3.00	_____
Game of Life 1960 Edition	_____ $20.00	_____ $11.00	_____ $3.00	_____
Game of Life 1991 Edition	_____ $7.00	_____ $5.00	_____ $1.00	_____
Game of Napoleon	_____ $18.00	_____ $13.00	_____ $3.00	_____
German Scrabble	_____ $11.00	_____ $8.00	_____ $2.00	_____
Guesstures	_____ $7.00	_____ $5.00	_____ $1.00	_____

See pages 11 & 12 for important information about properly valuing your donated items.

Games

Description	High* Good Condition	Average* Fair Condition	Low* Poor Condition	Total
Hi Ho Cherry-O	_____ $5.00	_____ $3.00	_____ $1.00	_____
Hungry Hungry Hippos	_____ $6.00	_____ $4.00	_____ $1.00	_____
Jenga	_____ $5.00	_____ $4.00	_____ $1.00	_____
Jeopardy	_____ $5.00	_____ $4.00	_____ $1.00	_____
Jeopardy 1960s Edition	_____ $5.00	_____ $4.00	_____ $1.00	_____
Laverne and Shirley	_____ $7.00	_____ $5.00	_____ $1.00	_____
LeMans Racing	_____ $29.00	_____ $25.00	_____ $5.00	_____
Memory	_____ $7.00	_____ $5.00	_____ $1.00	_____
Monopoly	_____ $23.00	_____ $11.00	_____ $3.00	_____
Mousetrap	_____ $7.00	_____ $5.00	_____ $1.00	_____
Mystery at Hogwarts	_____ $14.00	_____ $12.00	_____ $2.00	_____
Nellie Bly	_____ $87.00	_____ $64.00	_____ $13.00	_____
Newly Wed Game	_____ $8.00	_____ $6.00	_____ $2.00	_____
Operation	_____ $8.00	_____ $5.00	_____ $1.00	_____
Operation 1965	_____ $9.00	_____ $6.00	_____ $2.00	_____
Outburst	_____ $4.00	_____ $3.00	_____ $1.00	_____
Outburst II	_____ $8.00	_____ $6.00	_____ $1.00	_____
Outburst Junior	_____ $5.00	_____ $3.00	_____ $1.00	_____
Pictionary	_____ $8.00	_____ $5.00	_____ $2.00	_____
Pictionary 1st Edition	_____ $7.00	_____ $5.00	_____ $1.00	_____
Pictionary Party Edition	_____ $27.00	_____ $19.00	_____ $4.00	_____
Risk 40th Anniversary	_____ $61.00	_____ $45.00	_____ $9.00	_____
RSVP Scrabble	_____ $6.00	_____ $4.00	_____ $1.00	_____
Scattergories	_____ $8.00	_____ $6.00	_____ $2.00	_____
Scattergories Junior	_____ $5.00	_____ $3.00	_____ $1.00	_____
Scotland Yard	_____ $7.00	_____ $6.00	_____ $1.00	_____
Scrabble	_____ $14.00	_____ $6.00	_____ $2.00	_____
Scrabble 1953	_____ $8.00	_____ $5.00	_____ $1.00	_____
Scrabble 1966	_____ $16.00	_____ $10.00	_____ $3.00	_____
Scrabble 1976	_____ $9.00	_____ $5.00	_____ $2.00	_____
Scrabble Junior	_____ $7.00	_____ $4.00	_____ $1.00	_____
Scruples	_____ $5.00	_____ $4.00	_____ $1.00	_____
Sherlock Holmes	_____ $3.00	_____ $2.00	_____ $1.00	_____

See pages 11 & 12 for important information about properly valuing your donated items.

Games

Description	High* Good Condition	Average* Fair Condition	Low* Poor Condition	Total
Showdown Yahtzee	_____ $6.00	_____ $4.00	_____ $1.00	_____
Six Million Dollar Man	_____ $8.00	_____ $5.00	_____ $2.00	_____
Sleuth	_____ $21.00	_____ $15.00	_____ $3.00	_____
Stratego	_____ $11.00	_____ $7.00	_____ $2.00	_____
Survivor	_____ $7.00	_____ $6.00	_____ $1.00	_____
Taboo	_____ $10.00	_____ $8.00	_____ $2.00	_____
Travel Edition Scrabble	_____ $23.00	_____ $15.00	_____ $4.00	_____
Triple Yahtzee	_____ $6.00	_____ $4.00	_____ $1.00	_____
Trivial Pursuit				
10th Anniversary	_____ $13.00	_____ $9.00	_____ $2.00	_____
Genus I	_____ $14.00	_____ $8.00	_____ $2.00	_____
Genus IV	_____ $16.00	_____ $12.00	_____ $3.00	_____
Junior	_____ $8.00	_____ $6.00	_____ $1.00	_____
Master Baby Boomer	_____ $11.00	_____ $8.00	_____ $2.00	_____
Millennium	_____ $22.00	_____ $16.00	_____ $4.00	_____
Music Edition	_____ $4.00	_____ $3.00	_____ $1.00	_____
TV Edition	_____ $11.00	_____ $8.00	_____ $2.00	_____
Young Player	_____ $8.00	_____ $6.00	_____ $1.00	_____
Master Genus Ed	_____ $6.00	_____ $4.00	_____ $1.00	_____
Trivial Pursuit Master All American	_____ $15.00	_____ $12.00	_____ $3.00	_____
Trouble	_____ $7.00	_____ $5.00	_____ $1.00	_____
Truth or Dare Jenga	_____ $24.00	_____ $18.00	_____ $4.00	_____
Twister	_____ $7.00	_____ $5.00	_____ $1.00	_____
Twister 1960s	_____ $10.00	_____ $7.00	_____ $2.00	_____
Twister 1970s	_____ $14.00	_____ $7.00	_____ $2.00	_____
Waterloo	_____ $44.00	_____ $11.00	_____ $7.00	_____
Wheel of Fortune				
Deluxe	_____ $6.50	_____ $4.00	_____ $1.00	_____
Regular	_____ $5.00	_____ $3.00	_____ $1.00	_____
Who Wants to be a Millionaire	_____ $8.00	_____ $5.00	_____ $2.00	_____
Word Yahtzee	_____ $9.00	_____ $5.00	_____ $2.00	_____
Yacht Race	_____ $37.00	_____ $23.00	_____ $6.00	_____

See pages 11 & 12 for important information about properly valuing your donated items.

Games

Description	High* Good Condition		Average* Fair Condition		Low* Poor Condition		Total
Yahtzee							
40th Anniversary	_____	$9.00	_____	$6.00	_____	$2.00	_____
Deluxe Edition	_____	$9.00	_____	$7.00	_____	$2.00	_____
Junior	_____	$6.00	_____	$4.00	_____	$1.00	_____
Original	_____	$8.00	_____	$5.00	_____	$2.00	_____
Computer Games							
Macintosh	_____	$13.00	_____	$9.00	_____	$3.00	_____
PC	_____	$13.00	_____	$9.00	_____	$3.00	_____
Video Games							
Cartridges	_____	$15.00	_____	$5.00	_____	$1.00	_____
TOTAL GAMES						$	

See pages 11 & 12 for important information about properly valuing your donated items.

Toys

Description	High* Good Condition	Average* Fair Condition	Low* Poor Condition	Total
Electronic Pets				
iPuppy	_____ $15.00	_____ $11.00	_____ $3.00	_____
Fisher Price				
Briarberry				
Berryellen	_____ $12.00	_____ $10.00	_____ $2.00	_____
Berryellen and Berrykate	_____ $24.00	_____ $20.00	_____ $4.00	_____
Berryjustin	_____ $14.00	_____ $8.00	_____ $2.00	_____
Berrykate	_____ $13.00	_____ $5.00	_____ $2.00	_____
Berrykris and Sleigh	_____ $16.00	_____ $8.00	_____ $3.00	_____
Berrylouise and Case	_____ $23.00	_____ $15.00	_____ $4.00	_____
Birthday Party	_____ $8.00	_____ $4.00	_____ $2.00	_____
Chair-Bed	_____ $13.00	_____ $7.00	_____ $2.00	_____
Cradle	_____ $16.00	_____ $7.00	_____ $3.00	_____
Dining Room	_____ $15.00	_____ $9.00	_____ $3.00	_____
Hannahberry	_____ $15.00	_____ $9.00	_____ $3.00	_____
Highchair	_____ $15.00	_____ $9.00	_____ $3.00	_____
Highchair and Cradle	_____ $24.00	_____ $19.00	_____ $4.00	_____
Kitchen	_____ $15.00	_____ $9.00	_____ $3.00	_____
Rocker With Mouse	_____ $13.00	_____ $8.00	_____ $2.00	_____
Swing	_____ $24.00	_____ $12.00	_____ $4.00	_____
Tea Party	_____ $10.00	_____ $4.00	_____ $2.00	_____
Wardrobe	_____ $13.00	_____ $6.00	_____ $2.00	_____
Wedding	_____ $20.00	_____ $6.00	_____ $3.00	_____
Dollhouse				
Backyard Fun	_____ $16.00	_____ $10.00	_____ $3.00	_____
Candy Shop and Dance Studio	_____ $14.00	_____ $4.00	_____ $2.00	_____
Family Camping	_____ $21.00	_____ $12.00	_____ $3.00	_____
Holiday Fun	_____ $10.00	_____ $4.00	_____ $2.00	_____
Huge Lot (20+ pieces)	_____ $35.00	_____ $17.00	_____ $6.00	_____

See pages 11 & 12 for important information about properly valuing your donated items.

Toys

Description	High* Good Condition	Average* Fair Condition	Low* Poor Condition	Total
Great Adventures				
Bandit Pirates	_____ $9.00	_____ $7.00	_____ $2.00	_____
Blue Beard	_____ $7.00	_____ $4.00	_____ $1.00	_____
Pirate Pirates	_____ $14.00	_____ $4.00	_____ $2.00	_____
Pirate Ship Sea Serpent	_____ $12.00	_____ $3.00	_____ $2.00	_____
Kitchens, Play Food and Play Dishes				
Pie Surprise Dessert	_____ $13.00	_____ $6.00	_____ $2.00	_____
Speedy Spaghetti	_____ $10.00	_____ $5.00	_____ $2.00	_____
Little People				
Accessories	_____ $15.00	_____ $8.00	_____ $3.00	_____
A-Frame House	_____ $18.00	_____ $10.00	_____ $3.00	_____
Airport	_____ $24.00	_____ $10.00	_____ $4.00	_____
Baby with Bib	_____ $10.00	_____ $6.00	_____ $2.00	_____
Baby Zoo Animals	_____ $17.00	_____ $9.00	_____ $3.00	_____
Big Top Balancing Bear	_____ $9.00	_____ $6.00	_____ $2.00	_____
Christmas Village	_____ $30.00	_____ $14.00	_____ $5.00	_____
Chunky Animals	_____ $10.00	_____ $5.00	_____ $2.00	_____
Circus Train	_____ $16.00	_____ $8.00	_____ $3.00	_____
Circus Train Animals	_____ $14.00	_____ $8.00	_____ $2.00	_____
Clown	_____ $8.00	_____ $5.00	_____ $2.00	_____
Family Fun Jet	_____ $24.00	_____ $13.00	_____ $4.00	_____
Farm	_____ $13.00	_____ $7.00	_____ $2.00	_____
Ferris Wheel	_____ $20.00	_____ $10.00	_____ $3.00	_____
Figures	_____ $11.00	_____ $7.00	_____ $2.00	_____
Fireman	_____ $14.00	_____ $7.00	_____ $3.00	_____
Floaty Boat	_____ $9.00	_____ $5.00	_____ $2.00	_____
Garage	_____ $21.00	_____ $11.00	_____ $3.00	_____
House	_____ $16.00	_____ $8.00	_____ $3.00	_____
Mainstreet Phone	_____ $10.00	_____ $5.00	_____ $2.00	_____
Nativity	_____ $91.00	_____ $55.00	_____ $14.00	_____
Olympic Stars	_____ $11.00	_____ $6.00	_____ $2.00	_____

See pages 11 & 12 for important information about properly valuing your donated items.

Toys

Description	High* Good Condition	Average* Fair Condition	Low* Poor Condition	Total
Pets	_____ $10.00	_____ $6.00	_____ $2.00	_____
Play and Go Sets	_____ $34.00	_____ $17.00	_____ $5.00	_____
Playground	_____ $10.00	_____ $6.00	_____ $2.00	_____
Prince and Princess	_____ $11.00	_____ $7.00	_____ $2.00	_____
Safari Mountain	_____ $13.00	_____ $8.00	_____ $2.00	_____
Sarah Doll	_____ $10.00	_____ $6.00	_____ $2.00	_____
School Bus	_____ $11.00	_____ $6.00	_____ $2.00	_____
Sea Plane	_____ $8.00	_____ $5.00	_____ $1.00	_____
Sesame Street House	_____ $15.00	_____ $9.00	_____ $3.00	_____
Sewing Machine	_____ $6.00	_____ $5.00	_____ $1.00	_____
Space Ship	_____ $10.00	_____ $7.00	_____ $2.00	_____
Swimming Pool	_____ $14.00	_____ $7.00	_____ $3.00	_____
Taxi	_____ $14.00	_____ $9.00	_____ $2.00	_____
Train	_____ $14.00	_____ $8.00	_____ $2.00	_____
Western Town	_____ $19.00	_____ $12.00	_____ $3.00	_____
Zoo	_____ $18.00	_____ $10.00	_____ $3.00	_____
Miscellaneous				
Cassette Player	_____ $11.00	_____ $8.00	_____ $2.00	_____
Band Toys	_____ $8.00	_____ $5.00	_____ $1.00	_____
Happy Apple Chime Rattle	_____ $7.00	_____ $5.00	_____ $1.00	_____
Jalopy	_____ $7.00	_____ $4.00	_____ $1.00	_____
Lil Snoopy	_____ $7.00	_____ $4.00	_____ $1.00	_____
Mini Copter	_____ $10.00	_____ $5.00	_____ $2.00	_____
Musical Tick Tock Clock	_____ $16.00	_____ $9.00	_____ $3.00	_____
Puffalump Christmas Mouse	_____ $4.00	_____ $3.00	_____ $1.00	_____
Spiral Speedway	_____ $8.00	_____ $4.00	_____ $1.00	_____
Rescue Heroes				
Billy Blazes	_____ $18.00	_____ $13.00	_____ $3.00	_____
Billy Blazes Launch Force	_____ $15.00	_____ $12.00	_____ $3.00	_____

See pages 11 & 12 for important information about properly valuing your donated items.

Toys

Description	High* Good Condition	Average* Fair Condition	Low* Poor Condition	Total
Cliff Hanger	___ $18.00	___ $13.00	___ $3.00	___
Color Activity Books	___ $7.00	___ $5.00	___ $1.00	___
Command Center	___ $33.00	___ $25.00	___ $5.00	___
Command Center, Video and Rocky	___ $26.00	___ $20.00	___ $4.00	___
FDNY Billy Blazes	___ $17.00	___ $14.00	___ $3.00	___
Gil Gripper	___ $14.00	___ $10.00	___ $2.00	___
Nemo the Dolphin	___ $15.00	___ $11.00	___ $3.00	___
Rocky	___ $17.00	___ $10.00	___ $3.00	___
Roger Houston	___ $18.00	___ $13.00	___ $3.00	___
Sam Sparks	___ $13.00	___ $10.00	___ $2.00	___
Sandy Beach	___ $12.00	___ $9.00	___ $2.00	___
Smokey	___ $14.00	___ $10.00	___ $2.00	___
Video	___ $12.00	___ $8.00	___ $2.00	___
Video and Toothbrushes	___ $11.00	___ $9.00	___ $2.00	___
Wendy Waters	___ $16.00	___ $11.00	___ $3.00	___
Windchill	___ $12.00	___ $9.00	___ $2.00	___
Roleplay				
Medical Kit	___ $7.00	___ $4.00	___ $1.00	___
Play Tools	___ $8.00	___ $5.00	___ $1.00	___
Harry Potter				
Bertie Botts Beans	___ $8.00	___ $5.00	___ $2.00	___
Harry Potter Poster	___ $12.00	___ $6.00	___ $2.00	___
Magnet	___ $6.00	___ $3.00	___ $1.00	___
Movie Poster	___ $10.00	___ $6.00	___ $2.00	___
Mug				
Harry and Hagrid	___ $8.00	___ $6.00	___ $2.00	___
Harry and Hedwig	___ $8.00	___ $5.00	___ $2.00	___
Harry and Key	___ $8.00	___ $6.00	___ $2.00	___
Harry and Snitch	___ $7.00	___ $5.00	___ $1.00	___
Plush Hedwig	___ $24.00	___ $17.00	___ $4.00	___

*See pages 11 & 12 for important information about properly valuing your donated items.

Toys

Description	High* Good Condition	Average* Fair Condition	Low* Poor Condition	Total
Quidditch Card Game	_____ $5.00	_____ $3.00	_____ $1.00	_____
Quidditch Poster	_____ $7.00	_____ $5.00	_____ $1.00	_____
Quidditch Puzzle	_____ $8.00	_____ $6.00	_____ $2.00	_____
Snapes Potion Lab	_____ $33.00	_____ $28.00	_____ $5.00	_____
Sorceror Stone				
Bertie Botts	_____ $2.00	_____ $1.00	_____ $0.50	_____
Fluffy	_____ $2.00	_____ $1.00	_____ $0.50	_____
Flying Keys	_____ $1.50	_____ $1.00	_____ $0.50	_____
Golden Snitch	_____ $21.00	_____ $18.00	_____ $3.00	_____
Green Spells	_____ $2.00	_____ $1.00	_____ $0.50	_____
Gryffindor	_____ $2.00	_____ $1.00	_____ $0.50	_____
Harrys Glasses	_____ $2.00	_____ $1.00	_____ $0.50	_____
Hufflepuff	_____ $2.00	_____ $1.00	_____ $0.50	_____
Mrs. Norris	_____ $2.00	_____ $1.00	_____ $0.50	_____
Norbert	_____ $2.00	_____ $1.00	_____ $0.50	_____
Philosophers	_____ $12.00	_____ $6.00	_____ $2.00	_____
Potions	_____ $1.50	_____ $1.00	_____ $0.50	_____
Red Hedwig	_____ $2.00	_____ $1.50	_____ $1.00	_____
Ron	_____ $1.50	_____ $1.00	_____ $0.50	_____
Scabbers	_____ $2.00	_____ $1.00	_____ $0.50	_____
Slytherin	_____ $2.00	_____ $1.00	_____ $0.50	_____
Snape	_____ $2.00	_____ $1.00	_____ $0.50	_____
Sorting Hat	_____ $2.00	_____ $1.00	_____ $0.50	_____
Yellow Ravenclaw	_____ $1.50	_____ $1.00	_____ $0.50	_____
You Know Who	_____ $2.00	_____ $1.00	_____ $0.50	_____
Stationary Set	_____ $6.00	_____ $5.00	_____ $1.00	_____
Storyteller Figurine				
Dumbledore	_____ $24.00	_____ $18.00	_____ $4.00	_____
Fluffy	_____ $12.00	_____ $8.00	_____ $2.00	_____
Harry	_____ $17.00	_____ $11.00	_____ $3.00	_____
Hedwig	_____ $7.00	_____ $5.00	_____ $1.00	_____

See pages 11 & 12 for important information about properly valuing your donated items.

Toys

Description	High* Good Condition	Average* Fair Condition	Low* Poor Condition	Total
Hermione	_____ $13.00	_____ $9.00	_____ $2.00	_____
Ron Weasley	_____ $9.00	_____ $6.00	_____ $2.00	_____
Through the Trapdoor	_____ $15.00	_____ $12.00	_____ $3.00	_____
Wand	_____ $14.00	_____ $7.00	_____ $2.00	_____

Little Tikes

Cars and Trucks

Description	High* Good Condition	Average* Fair Condition	Low* Poor Condition	Total
18 Wheeler	_____ $20.00	_____ $13.00	_____ $3.00	_____
Adventure Mountain Raceway	_____ $95.00	_____ $73.00	_____ $15.00	_____
Dump Truck	_____ $8.00	_____ $5.00	_____ $1.00	_____
Front Endloader	_____ $9.00	_____ $5.00	_____ $2.00	_____
Red 4x4 Truck	_____ $10.00	_____ $6.00	_____ $2.00	_____

Dollhouse

Description	High* Good Condition	Average* Fair Condition	Low* Poor Condition	Total
Baby Buggy	_____ $5.00	_____ $4.00	_____ $1.00	_____
Blue Roof Dollhouse with Accessories	_____ $30.00	_____ $15.00	_____ $5.00	_____
Country Kitchen	_____ $9.00	_____ $7.00	_____ $2.00	_____
Cozy Coupe	_____ $5.00	_____ $4.00	_____ $1.00	_____
Desk	_____ $6.00	_____ $4.00	_____ $1.00	_____
Desk and Chair	_____ $6.00	_____ $4.00	_____ $1.00	_____
Family	_____ $10.00	_____ $6.00	_____ $2.00	_____
Grand Mansion	_____ $31.00	_____ $11.00	_____ $10.00	_____
Grandparents	_____ $17.00	_____ $9.00	_____ $3.00	_____
Kitchen	_____ $7.00	_____ $4.00	_____ $1.00	_____
Mattress	_____ $5.00	_____ $4.00	_____ $1.00	_____
Mini Van	_____ $6.00	_____ $5.00	_____ $1.00	_____
Nursery	_____ $12.00	_____ $8.00	_____ $2.00	_____
Picnic Table	_____ $4.00	_____ $2.00	_____ $1.00	_____
Slippery Slide	_____ $5.00	_____ $4.00	_____ $1.00	_____
Swimming Pool	_____ $5.00	_____ $4.00	_____ $1.00	_____
Teddy Bear	_____ $9.00	_____ $5.00	_____ $2.00	_____
Turtle Sandbox	_____ $12.00	_____ $9.00	_____ $2.00	_____

See pages 11 & 12 for important information about properly valuing your donated items.

Toys

Description	High* Good Condition		Average* Fair Condition		Low* Poor Condition		Total
Vacuum Cleaner	____	$7.00	____	$5.00	____	$1.00	____
Furniture							
Creative Art Studio Desk	____	$49.00	____	$22.00	____	$8.00	____
Football Toy Box	____	$57.00	____	$37.00	____	$9.00	____
Tire Toy Box	____	$48.00	____	$35.00	____	$8.00	____
Infant							
Activity Garden	____	$58.00	____	$37.00	____	$9.00	____
Baby Tap-a-Tune Piano	____	$5.00	____	$3.00	____	$1.00	____
Nesting Farm Animals	____	$8.00	____	$6.00	____	$1.00	____
Kitchens							
Hutch with Dishes	____	$31.00	____	$29.00	____	$5.00	____
Kitchen	____	$27.00	____	$13.00	____	$4.00	____
Refrigerator	____	$20.00	____	$10.00	____	$3.00	____
Preschool							
Choo Choo Zoo Train	____	$8.00	____	$6.00	____	$1.00	____
Drum	____	$6.00	____	$4.00	____	$1.00	____
Toddle Totmobile Space Set	____	$11.00	____	$5.00	____	$2.00	____
Toddle Tots School Bus	____	$8.00	____	$6.00	____	$1.00	____
Waffle Block Castle	____	$14.00	____	$10.00	____	$2.00	____
Waffle Blocks	____	$12.00	____	$8.00	____	$2.00	____
Ride-Ons							
Cozy Coupe	____	$13.00	____	$7.00	____	$2.00	____
Lion	____	$10.00	____	$6.00	____	$2.00	____
Toddler Wagon	____	$11.00	____	$8.00	____	$2.00	____
Zebra	____	$19.00	____	$13.00	____	$3.00	____
Roleplay							
Circular Saw	____	$6.00	____	$4.00	____	$1.00	____
Dishes and Bakeware	____	$16.00	____	$10.00	____	$3.00	____
Doll Bed	____	$15.00	____	$11.00	____	$3.00	____
Doll Stroller	____	$12.00	____	$8.00	____	$2.00	____

See pages 11 & 12 for important information about properly valuing your donated items.

Toys

Description	High* Good Condition	Average* Fair Condition	Low* Poor Condition	Total
Happy Pumper Gas Pump	_____ $8.00	_____ $6.00	_____ $2.00	_____
Play Money	_____ $9.00	_____ $5.00	_____ $2.00	_____
Shopping Cart	_____ $16.00	_____ $12.00	_____ $3.00	_____
Victorian Tea Set Tray	_____ $9.00	_____ $3.00	_____ $2.00	_____
Wheelbarrow	_____ $13.00	_____ $10.00	_____ $2.00	_____
White Buggy	_____ $21.00	_____ $13.00	_____ $4.00	_____
Workbench With Tools and Chair	_____ $20.00	_____ $9.00	_____ $3.00	_____
Seasonal				
Turtle Sandbox	_____ $12.00	_____ $9.00	_____ $2.00	_____
Miscellaneous				
Puzzles	_____ $5.00	_____ $1.00	_____ $0.50	_____
Stuffed Animal				
Large	_____ $12.00	_____ $4.00	_____ $1.00	_____
Small	_____ $8.00	_____ $3.00	_____ $1.00	_____
TOTAL TOYS			$	

See pages 11 & 12 for important information about properly valuing your donated items.

Custom Item Donations

ItsDeductible™ contains thousands of item values for the most commonly donated items. However, it is likely that you will be donating some items which are not included in this workbook.

The following form allows you to track all of your **custom item dona-tions.**

When creating a custom item donation, you will be responsible for deter-mining the value of the item. There are several common methods that you might use:

- Determine the value of comparable items at a <u>Thrift or Consignment Shop</u>.
- Have an <u>Appraisal</u> done on your item. You will typically only want to do this on very expense items like Jewelry or Art.
- Use a <u>Catalog</u> for collectible items such as stamps, coins, or baseball cards.
- Utilize <u>Comparable Sales</u> for things like real estate or other valuable assets.

For items valued at over $500, try to also include the original purchase date and value for your records.

Custom Item Donations

Item Description	
Condition	❏ **Good** ❏ **Fair** ❏ **Poor**
Quantity	
Value	$
Method of Valuation	
Complete the following only if the Item Value is greater than $500	
Date Acquired	
Cost or Adjusted Basis	
How was this Item Acquired?	

Item Description	
Condition	❏ **Good** ❏ **Fair** ❏ **Poor**
Quantity	
Value	$
Method of Valuation	
Complete the following only if the Item Value is greater than $500	
Date Acquired	
Cost or Adjusted Basis	
How was this Item Acquired?	

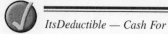

Custom Item Donations

Item Description	
Condition	❑ Good ❑ Fair ❑ Poor
Quantity	
Value	$
Method of Valuation	
Complete the following only if the Item Value is greater than $500	
Date Acquired	
Cost or Adjusted Basis	
How was this Item Acquired?	

Item Description	
Condition	❑ Good ❑ Fair ❑ Poor
Quantity	
Value	$
Method of Valuation	
Complete the following only if the Item Value is greater than $500	
Date Acquired	
Cost or Adjusted Basis	
How was this Item Acquired?	

Custom Item Donations

Item Description	
Condition	☐ **Good** ☐ **Fair** ☐ **Poor**
Quantity	
Value	$
Method of Valuation	

Complete the following only if the Item Value is greater than $500

Date Acquired	
Cost or Adjusted Basis	
How was this Item Acquired?	

Item Description	
Condition	☐ **Good** ☐ **Fair** ☐ **Poor**
Quantity	
Value	$
Method of Valuation	

Complete the following only if the Item Value is greater than $500

Date Acquired	
Cost or Adjusted Basis	
How was this Item Acquired?	

Custom Item Donations

Item Description	
Condition	❏ **Good** ❏ **Fair** ❏ **Poor**
Quantity	
Value	$
Method of Valuation	
Complete the following only if the Item Value is greater than $500	
Date Acquired	
Cost or Adjusted Basis	
How was this Item Acquired?	

Item Description	
Condition	❏ **Good** ❏ **Fair** ❏ **Poor**
Quantity	
Value	$
Method of Valuation	
Complete the following only if the Item Value is greater than $500	
Date Acquired	
Cost or Adjusted Basis	
How was this Item Acquired?	

Custom Item Donations

Item Description	
Condition	❑ **Good**　　❑ **Fair**　　❑ **Poor**
Quantity	
Value	$
Method of Valuation	
Complete the following only if the Item Value is greater than $500	
Date Acquired	
Cost or Adjusted Basis	
How was this Item Acquired?	

Item Description	
Condition	❑ **Good**　　❑ **Fair**　　❑ **Poor**
Quantity	
Value	$
Method of Valuation	
Complete the following only if the Item Value is greater than $500	
Date Acquired	
Cost or Adjusted Basis	
How was this Item Acquired?	

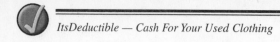

Custom Item Donations

Item Description	
Condition	☐ **Good** ☐ **Fair** ☐ **Poor**
Quantity	
Value	$
Method of Valuation	

Complete the following only if the Item Value is greater than $500

Date Acquired	
Cost or Adjusted Basis	
How was this Item Acquired?	

Item Description	
Condition	☐ **Good** ☐ **Fair** ☐ **Poor**
Quantity	
Value	$
Method of Valuation	

Complete the following only if the Item Value is greater than $500

Date Acquired	
Cost or Adjusted Basis	
How was this Item Acquired?	

Custom Item Donations

Item Description	
Condition	❏ **Good**　　❏ **Fair**　　❏ **Poor**
Quantity	
Value	$
Method of Valuation	
Complete the following only if the Item Value is greater than $500	
Date Acquired	
Cost or Adjusted Basis	
How was this Item Acquired?	

Item Description	
Condition	❏ **Good**　　❏ **Fair**　　❏ **Poor**
Quantity	
Value	$
Method of Valuation	
Complete the following only if the Item Value is greater than $500	
Date Acquired	
Cost or Adjusted Basis	
How was this Item Acquired?	

Total Custom Item Donations	$

Mileage Expense Tracking

See the section in the front of this book called **Mileage Expenses** (page 14) to learn more about what kinds of mileage you can deduct on your taxes.

Description	Date	Miles Driven	Per Mile	Extended Total
Vacation Bible School	1/12/02	45	$.14	$ 6.30
Coaching Youth Sports	2/9/02	100	$.14	$ 14.00
Food Bank	1/12/02	50	$.14	$ 7.00
			$.14	$
			$.14	$
			$.14	$
			$.14	$
			$.14	$
			$.14	$
			$.14	$
			$.14	$
			$.14	$
			$.14	$
			$.14	$
			$.14	$
			$.14	$
			$.14	$
			$.14	$
			$.14	$

Mileage Expense Tracking

Description	Date	Miles Driven	Per Mile	Extended Total
			$.14	$
			$.14	$
			$.14	$
			$.14	$
			$.14	$
			$.14	$
			$.14	$
			$.14	$
			$.14	$
			$.14	$
			$.14	$
			$.14	$
			$.14	$
			$.14	$
			$.14	$
			$.14	$
			$.14	$
			$.14	$
			$.14	$
			$.14	$

Mileage Expense Tracking

Description	Date	Miles Driven	Per Mile	Extended Total
			$.14	$
			$.14	$
			$.14	$
			$.14	$
			$.14	$
			$.14	$
			$.14	$
			$.14	$
			$.14	$
			$.14	$
			$.14	$
			$.14	$
			$.14	$
			$.14	$
			$.14	$
			$.14	$
			$.14	$
			$.14	$
			$.14	$
			$.14	$

Mileage Expense Tracking

Description	Date	Miles Driven	Per Mile	Extended Total
			$.14	$
			$.14	$
			$.14	$
			$.14	$
			$.14	$
			$.14	$
			$.14	$
			$.14	$
			$.14	$
			$.14	$
			$.14	$
			$.14	$
			$.14	$
			$.14	$
			$.14	$
			$.14	$
			$.14	$
			$.14	$
			$.14	$
			$.14	$
Mileage Expenses Total				$

Monetary Donation Tracking

See the section in the front of this book called **Monetary Donations** (page 13) to learn more about making donations by cash, check, or credit card.

Description	Date	Check or Credit Card Number	Receipt?	Amount
American Cancer Society	1/5/ 2002	Check # 1234	❏ Yes ❏ No	$ 50.00
United Way	1/9/ 2002	Check # 1235	❏ Yes ❏ No	$ 25.00
Boy Scouts of America	2/2/ 2002	Check # 1236	❏ Yes ❏ No	$ 10.00
Red Cross	2/11/ 2002	Check # 1237	❏ Yes ❏ No	$ 25.00
			❏ Yes ❏ No	$
			❏ Yes ❏ No	$
			❏ Yes ❏ No	$
			❏ Yes ❏ No	$
			❏ Yes ❏ No	$
			❏ Yes ❏ No	$
			❏ Yes ❏ No	$
			❏ Yes ❏ No	$
			❏ Yes ❏ No	$
			❏ Yes ❏ No	$

Monetary Donation Tracking

Description	Date	Check or Credit Card Number	Receipt?	Amount
			❐ Yes ❐ No	$
			❐ Yes ❐ No	$
			❐ Yes ❐ No	$
			❐ Yes ❐ No	$
			❐ Yes ❐ No	$
			❐ Yes ❐ No	$
			❐ Yes ❐ No	$
			❐ Yes ❐ No	$
			❐ Yes ❐ No	$
			❐ Yes ❐ No	$
			❐ Yes ❐ No	$
			❐ Yes ❐ No	$
			❐ Yes ❐ No	$
			❐ Yes ❐ No	$
			❐ Yes ❐ No	$

Monetary Donation Tracking

Description	Date	Check or Credit Card Number	Receipt?	Amount
			❐ Yes ❐ No	$
			❐ Yes ❐ No	$
			❐ Yes ❐ No	$
			❐ Yes ❐ No	$
			❐ Yes ❐ No	$
			❐ Yes ❐ No	$
			❐ Yes ❐ No	$
			❐ Yes ❐ No	$
			❐ Yes ❐ No	$
			❐ Yes ❐ No	$
			❐ Yes ❐ No	$
			❐ Yes ❐ No	$
			❐ Yes ❐ No	$
			❐ Yes ❐ No	$
			❐ Yes ❐ No	$

Monetary Donation Tracking

Description	Date	Check or Credit Card Number	Receipt?	Amount
			❏ Yes ❏ No	$
			❏ Yes ❏ No	$
			❏ Yes ❏ No	$
			❏ Yes ❏ No	$
			❏ Yes ❏ No	$
			❏ Yes ❏ No	$
			❏ Yes ❏ No	$
			❏ Yes ❏ No	$
			❏ Yes ❏ No	$
			❏ Yes ❏ No	$
			❏ Yes ❏ No	$
			❏ Yes ❏ No	$
			❏ Yes ❏ No	$
			❏ Yes ❏ No	$
Total of all Monetary Donations				$

Out-of-Pocket Expenses Tracking

See the section in the front of this book called **Out-of-Pocket Expenses** (page 13) to learn more about what kinds of expenses are considered Out-of-Pocket donations.

Description	Date	Check or Credit Card Number	Receipt?	Amount
Church youth group pizza party	1/5/ 2002	Check # 1234	❏ Yes ❏ No	$ 50.25
Donuts for Boy Scouts of America	2/5/ 2002	Check # 1235	❏ Yes ❏ No	$ 8.99
Food purchase for the Food Bank	3/11/ 2002	Check # 1236	❏ Yes ❏ No	$ 19.99
			❏ Yes ❏ No	$
			❏ Yes ❏ No	$
			❏ Yes ❏ No	$
			❏ Yes ❏ No	$
			❏ Yes ❏ No	$
			❏ Yes ❏ No	$
			❏ Yes ❏ No	$
			❏ Yes ❏ No	$
			❏ Yes ❏ No	$
			❏ Yes ❏ No	$
			❏ Yes ❏ No	$

Out-of-Pocket Expenses Tracking

Description	Date	Check or Credit Card Number	Receipt?	Amount
			❏ Yes ❏ No	$
			❏ Yes ❏ No	$
			❏ Yes ❏ No	$
			❏ Yes ❏ No	$
			❏ Yes ❏ No	$
			❏ Yes ❏ No	$
			❏ Yes ❏ No	$
			❏ Yes ❏ No	$
			❏ Yes ❏ No	$
			❏ Yes ❏ No	$
			❏ Yes ❏ No	$
			❏ Yes ❏ No	$
			❏ Yes ❏ No	$
			❏ Yes ❏ No	$
			❏ Yes ❏ No	$

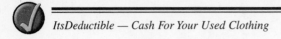

Out-of-Pocket Expenses Tracking

Description	Date	Check or Credit Card Number	Receipt?	Amount
			❒ Yes ❒ No	$
			❒ Yes ❒ No	$
			❒ Yes ❒ No	$
			❒ Yes ❒ No	$
			❒ Yes ❒ No	$
			❒ Yes ❒ No	$
			❒ Yes ❒ No	$
			❒ Yes ❒ No	$
			❒ Yes ❒ No	$
			❒ Yes ❒ No	$
			❒ Yes ❒ No	$
			❒ Yes ❒ No	$
			❒ Yes ❒ No	$
			❒ Yes ❒ No	$
			❒ Yes ❒ No	$

Out-of-Pocket Expenses Tracking

Description	Date	Check or Credit Card Number	Receipt?	Amount
			❏ Yes ❏ No	$
			❏ Yes ❏ No	$
			❏ Yes ❏ No	$
			❏ Yes ❏ No	$
			❏ Yes ❏ No	$
			❏ Yes ❏ No	$
			❏ Yes ❏ No	$
			❏ Yes ❏ No	$
			❏ Yes ❏ No	$
			❏ Yes ❏ No	$
			❏ Yes ❏ No	$
			❏ Yes ❏ No	$
			❏ Yes ❏ No	$
			❏ Yes ❏ No	$
Total of all Out-of-Pocket Donations				$

List of Charities to which you Donated

Fill out the information below for each charity you donate to. This will be useful during your income tax preparation.

Name of Charity				
Address				
Donation Dates				

Name of Charity				
Address				
Donation Dates				

Name of Charity				
Address				
Donation Dates				

Name of Charity				
Address				
Donation Dates				

Name of Charity				
Address				
Donation Dates				

List of Charities to which you Donated

Name of Charity	
Address	
Donation Dates	

Name of Charity	
Address	
Donation Dates	

Name of Charity	
Address	
Donation Dates	

Name of Charity	
Address	
Donation Dates	

Name of Charity	
Address	
Donation Dates	

List of Charities to which you Donated

Name of Charity				
Address				
Donation Dates				

Name of Charity				
Address				
Donation Dates				

Name of Charity				
Address				
Donation Dates				

Name of Charity				
Address				
Donation Dates				

Name of Charity				
Address				
Donation Dates				

List of Charities to which you Donated

Name of Charity				
Address				
Donation Dates				

Name of Charity				
Address				
Donation Dates				

Name of Charity				
Address				
Donation Dates				

Name of Charity				
Address				
Donation Dates				

Name of Charity				
Address				
Donation Dates				

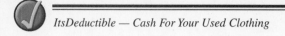

Tax Preparation Worksheet

Once you are ready to prepare your income taxes, you will need to know the total of your donations in each category. Total all your donations and record them below.

Category	Page #	Total Amount
Women's Clothing	26	$
Men's Clothing	31	$
Girl's Clothing	35	$
Boy's Clothing	39	$
Toddler's Clothing	42	$
Infant's Clothing	44	$
Women's Designer Clothing	49	$
Men's Designer Clothing	53	$
Jewelry	55	$
Baby Supplies	59	$
Electric Appliances - Small	69	$
Electric Appliances - Large	71	$
Entertainment	72	$
Furniture	75	$

Garden Tools	76	$
Household Miscellaneous	78	$
Linens	80	$
Pets	83	$
Tools	87	$
Exercise Equipment	89	$
Sporting Goods	98	$
Games	102	$
Toys	110	$
Total Item Donations		$
Total Custom Item Donations	119	$
Total Mileage Expenses	123	$
Total Monetary Donations	127	$
Total Out-of-Pocket Expenses	131	$
GRAND TOTAL		$
Estimated Federal and State Tax Rates Combined* (Use 33% if unsure)*		%
Approximate Tax Savings		$

*Visit your state tax website at: http://www.itsdeductible.com/html/help_statetax.shtml

Notes

Notes

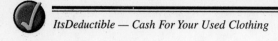
Notes

Notes

Notes

Notes

Notes

Register NOW to Activate Audit Protection!

Register your copy of ItsDeductible™ NOW to activate your Audit Protection Warranty *free of charge*. This warranty will take away any worries related to an IRS audit as it provides you with the following security:

- If the IRS questions the values assigned to your donations, we will provide the IRS with direct documentation supporting the fair-market-values provided by ItsDeductible™.
- If you ever receive any fines or penalties from the IRS that are associated with your donation and the fair-market-values assigned to your donations, we will pay those fines and penalties for you.

Your serial number will automatically be registered with Audit Protection Warranty. You do not need to keep any certificate or documentation on file. Just be sure to file your completed copy of ItsDeductible™ with your own personal tax records. *You will not receive any certificate or document in the mail related to Audit Protection upon receipt of registration.*

Income Dynamics hereby warrants that the fair-market-values contained in the ItsDeductible product were made in accordance with IRS regulations. Income Dynamics assumes responsibility for any interest and penalties imposed by the IRS and ultimately upheld by a court of competent jurisdiction in the event any value is challenged, and is proven to have been improperly determined. If any assigned value has been tampered with in any way, this warranty shall be null and void. Further, for this warranty to be effective, Income Dynamics must be notified immediately upon receipt of notice of any challenge of any valuation, and given full opportunity to participate in defending the same. This warranty extends only to the registered ItsDeductible owner only for the designated year. Any willful disregard for the copyright protection afforded this product, by reproducing or copying in any way will invalidate this warranty.

Complete the form below and mail to:

Income Dynamics, Inc., PO Box 540518, Omaha, NE 68154-0518

Or Visit www.ItsDeductible.com and Click on REGISTER NOW

Registration Card

ItsDeductible Serial # _____

Name _____

Address _____

City, State, Zip _____

Phone _____

Email _____

Keep Saving Tax Dollars!

Continue maximizing your tax savings with ItsDeductible™, available through firstnational.com and begin planning for tax year 2003.

ItsDeductible™

Online Edition

Learn about ItsDeductible Online Edition at:

www.itsdeductible.com/firstnational